How to Draw for Kids

A Step-by-Step Guided Drawing Book for Kids –
Learn to Draw Cute Stuff, Animals,
Magical Creatures, Cars and More!

CLEVER KIDDO PRESS

Thank you for getting our book!

If you find this drawing book fun and useful, we
would be very grateful if you post a short review on
Amazon! Your support does make a difference and we
read every review personally.

If you would like to leave a review, just head on
over to this book's Amazon page and click
"Write a customer review".

Thank you for your support!

How to Use this Book

1. Prepare a pencil, an eraser and paper to draw on.

2. Draw the black lines shown in the first step.

3. Continue to follow the instructions in each step and keep adding the black lines to complete the drawing.

4. If you get stuck in any step, you can trace the final step and then try drawing the image from the beginning.

5. Relax and have fun! You can do it!

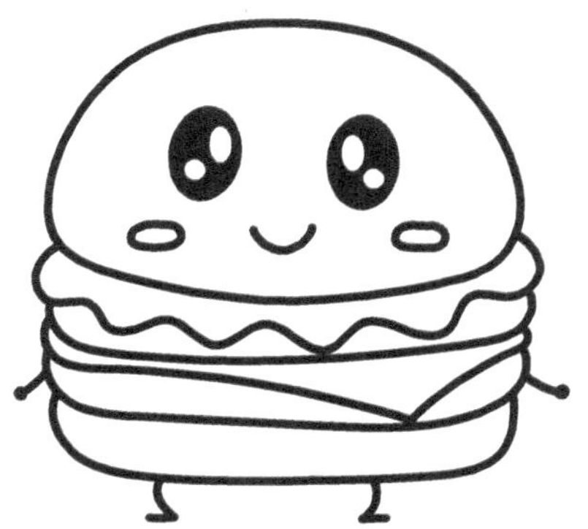

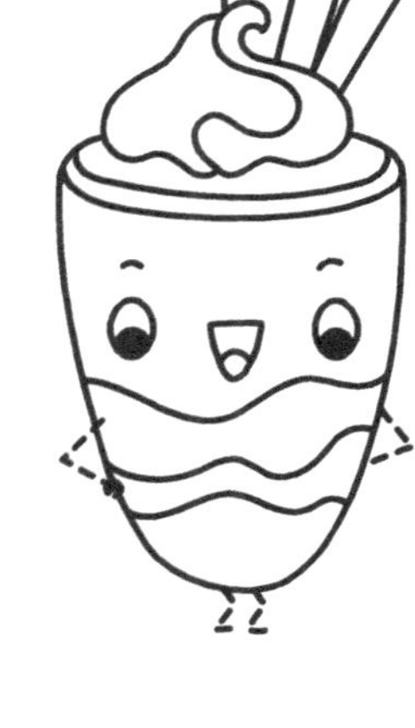

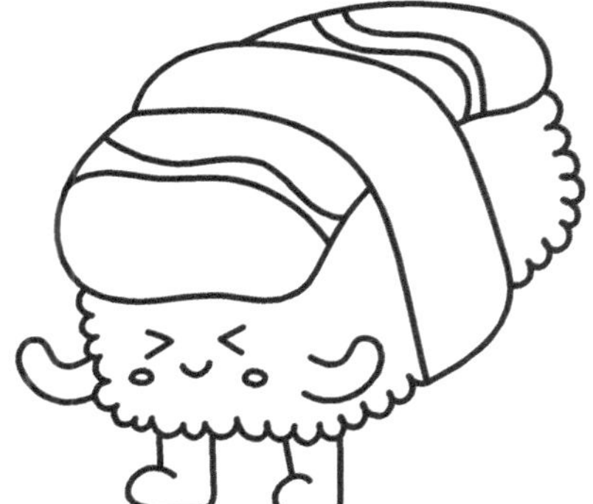

Cute
Food

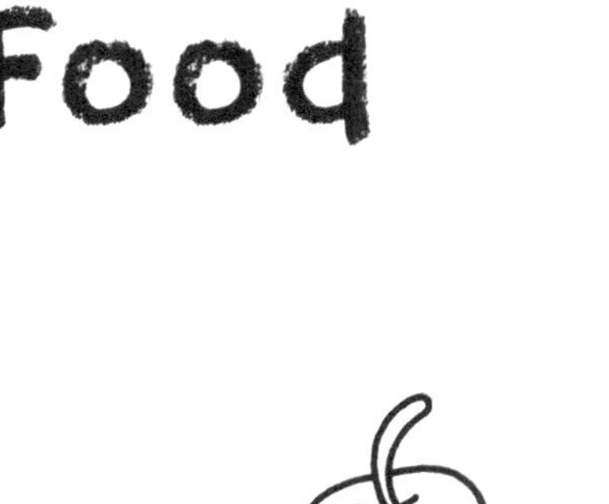

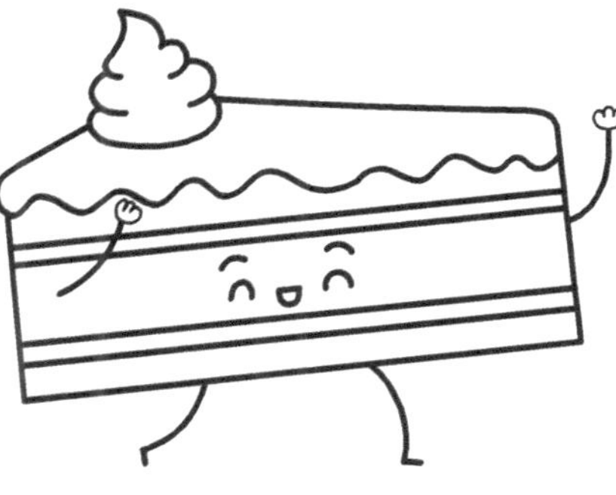

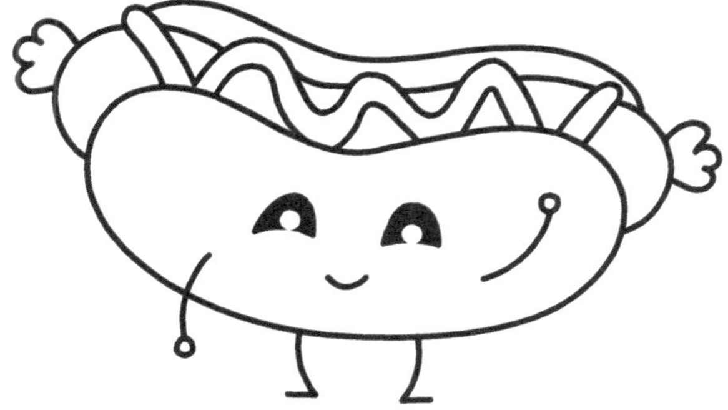

SUSHI

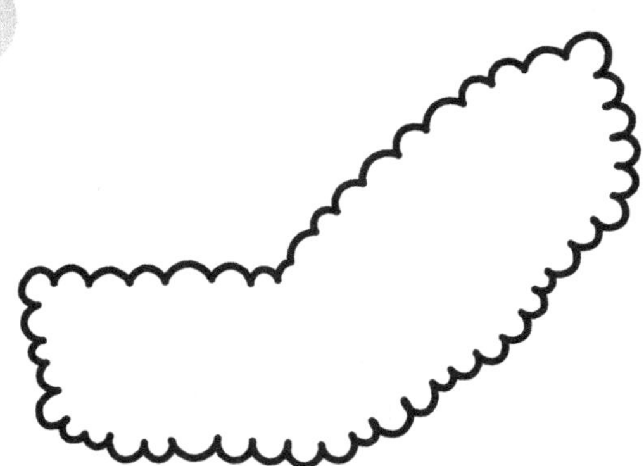

1

Draw a rectangular
cloud for the rice

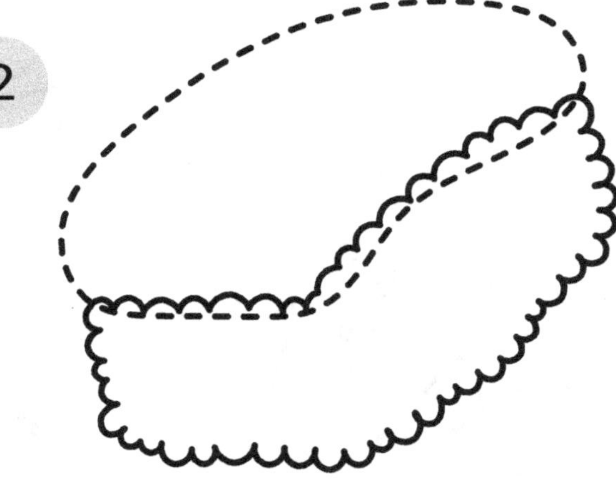

2

Draw another rectangle
for the meat

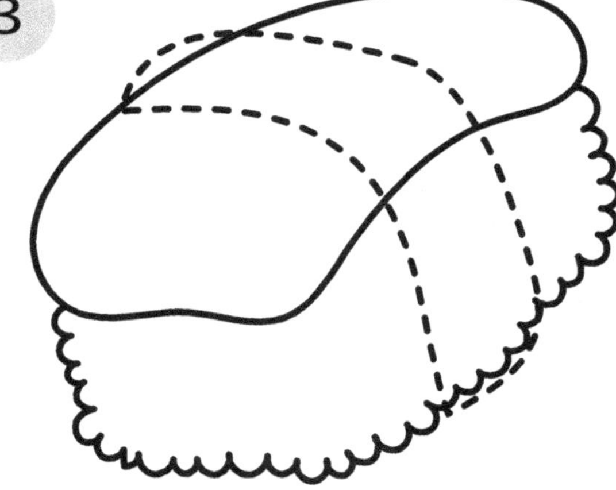

3

Make the sushi band

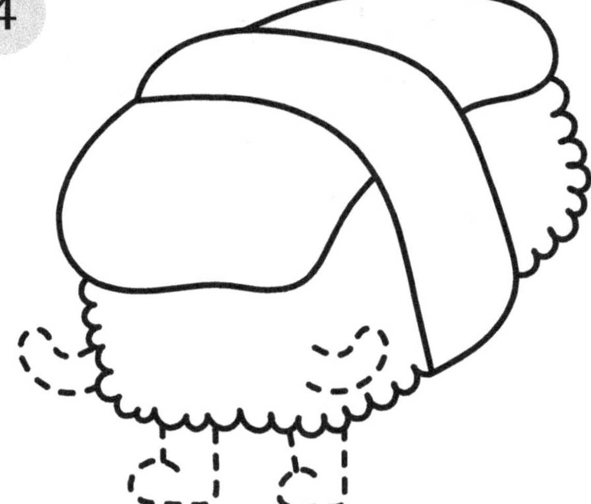

4

Make two small
legs and arms

5

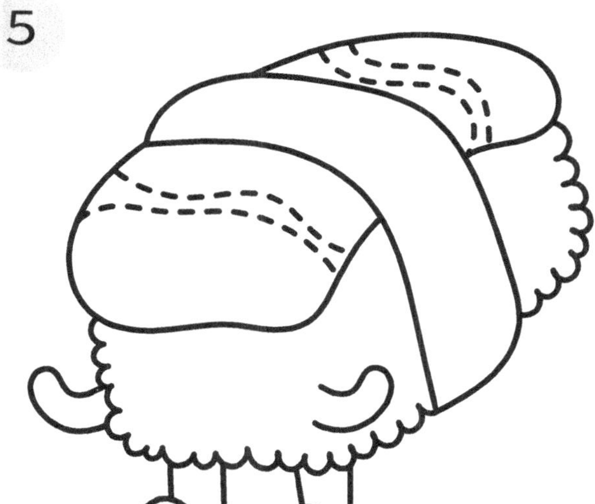

Draw a pattern to
decorate your sushi

6

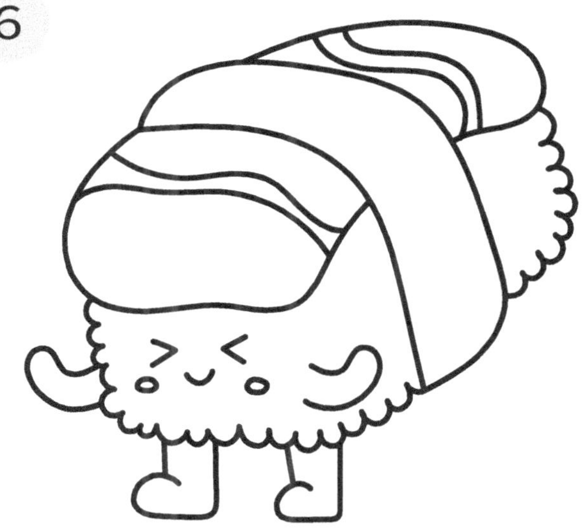

Make a cute little face
to complete it!

CUPCAKE

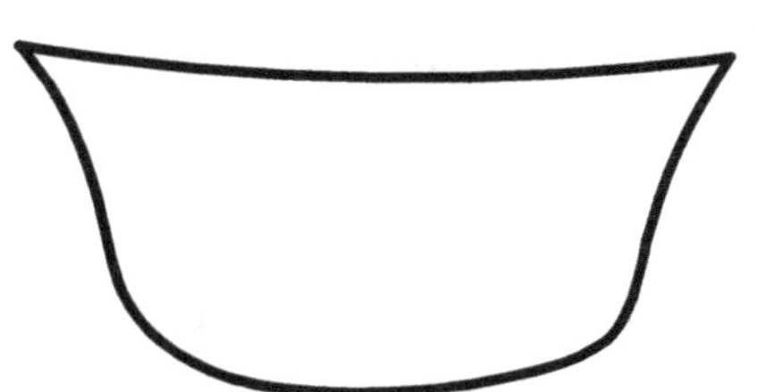

1

Draw a
rectangular cup

2

Make a cloud-shaped
cake on top

3

Draw a big, round cherry

4

Make the
rectangular wafers

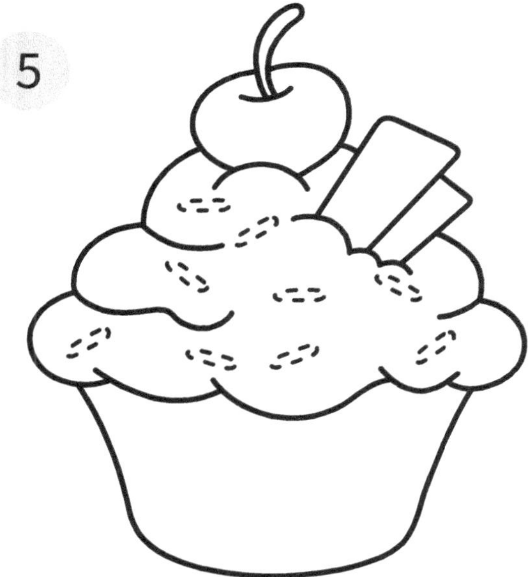

5

Draw a lot of sprinkles

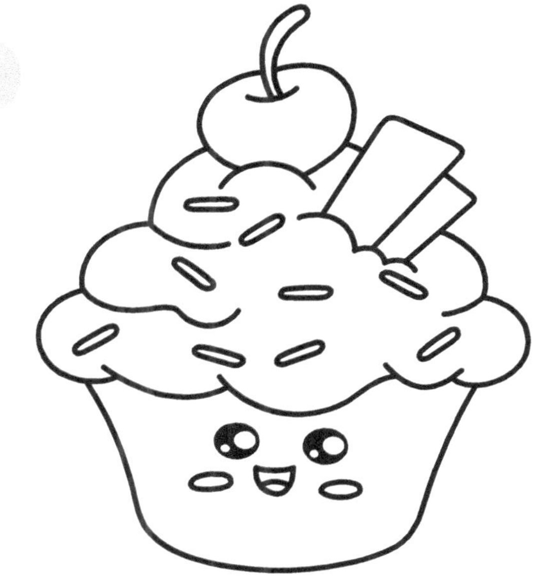

6

Make adorable eyes and face to complete your cupcake!

BURGER

1

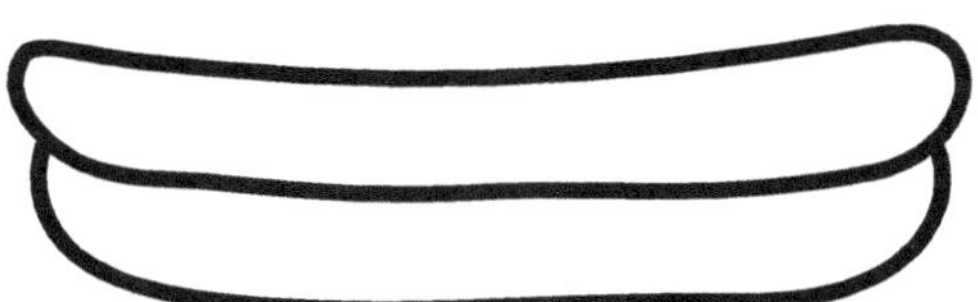

Draw two long layers

2

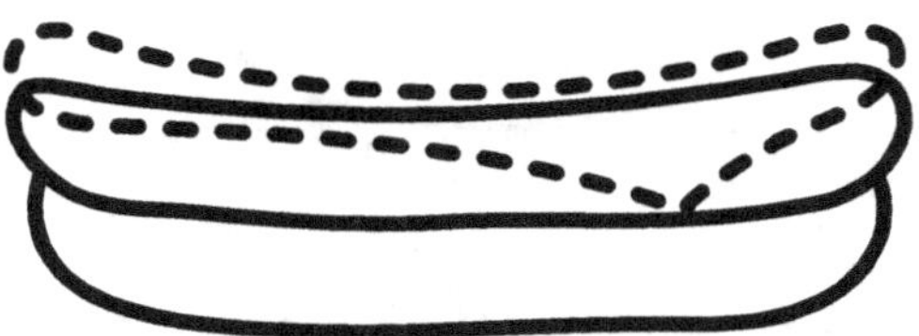

Draw another
layer of cheese

3

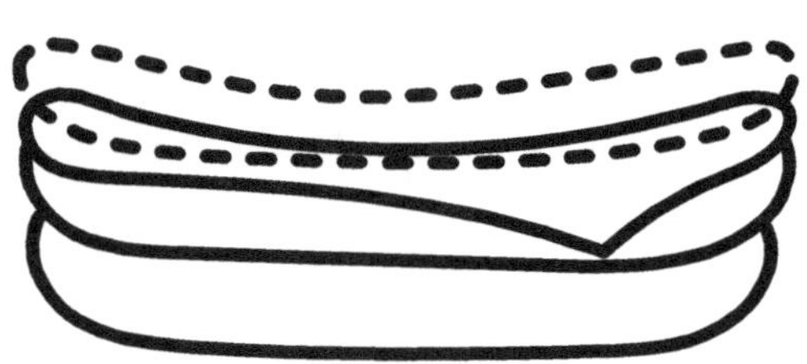

Make the tomato

4

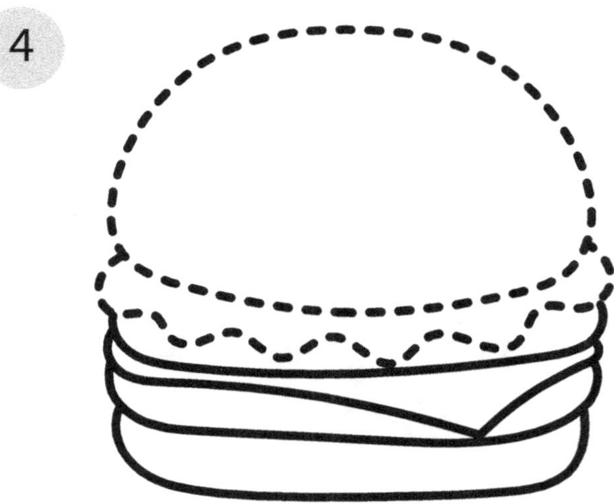

Top it with the bun and
a wavy leaf

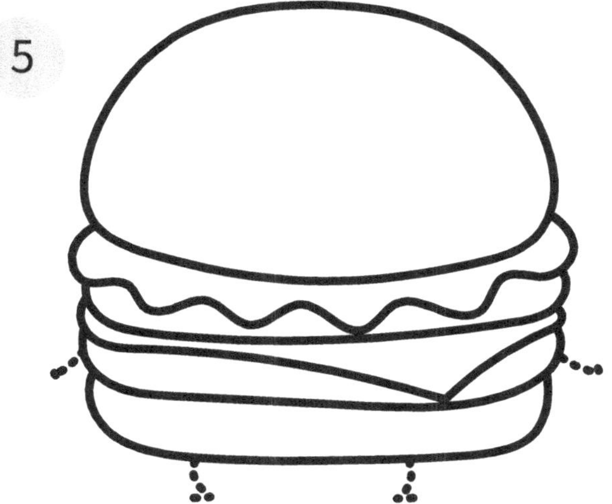

Draw cute, small
hands and legs

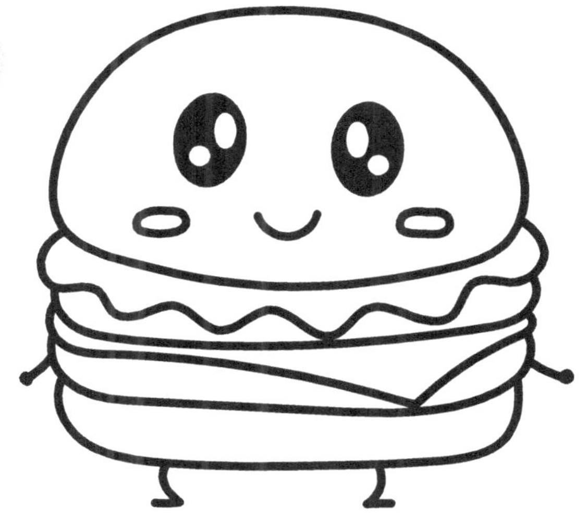

Draw the face to
complete your burger!

ICE CREAM

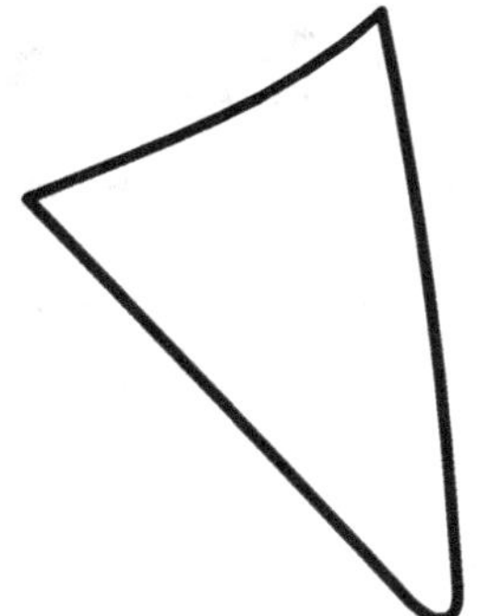

Make a triangular cone

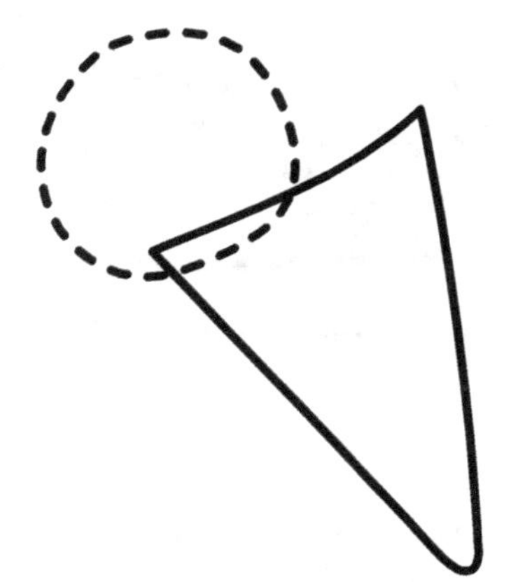

Draw a circular scoop

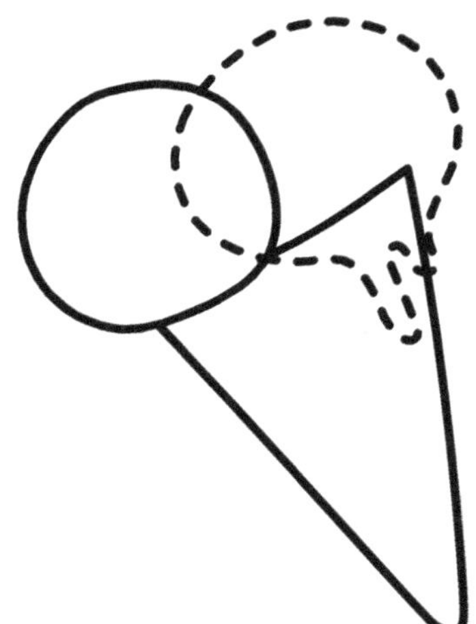

Draw another scoop

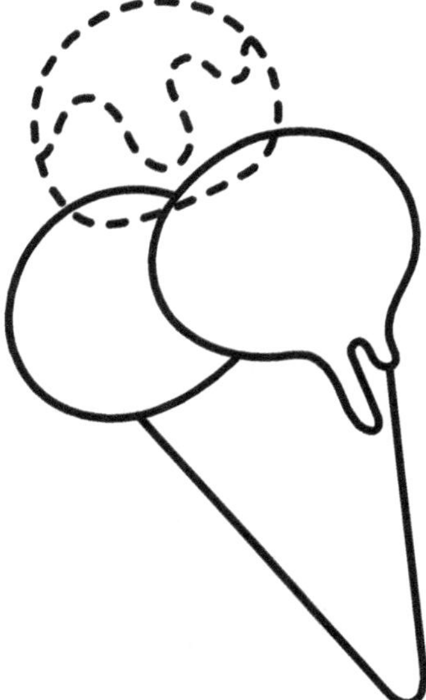

Draw one more
scoop on top with syrup

5

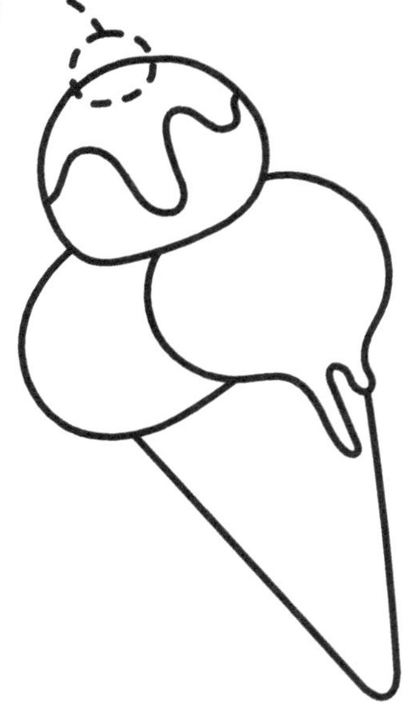

Draw a round cherry

6

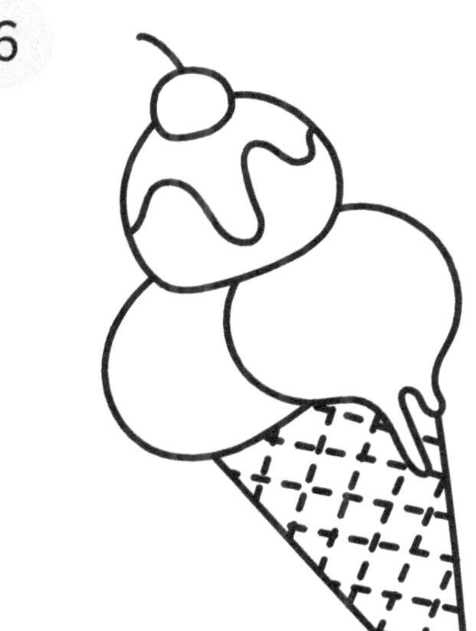

Decorate the cone to
make your ice cream!

MILK SHAKE

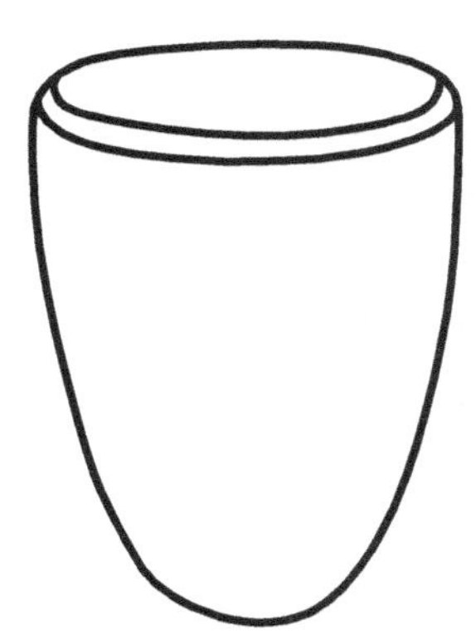

1

Draw a
round glass

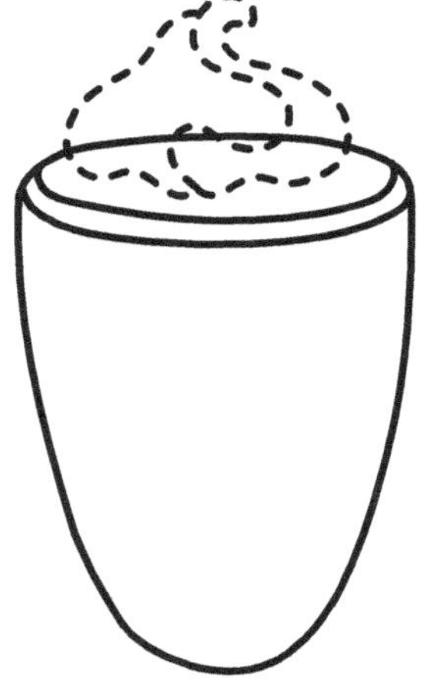

2

Now make a small
scoop of ice cream

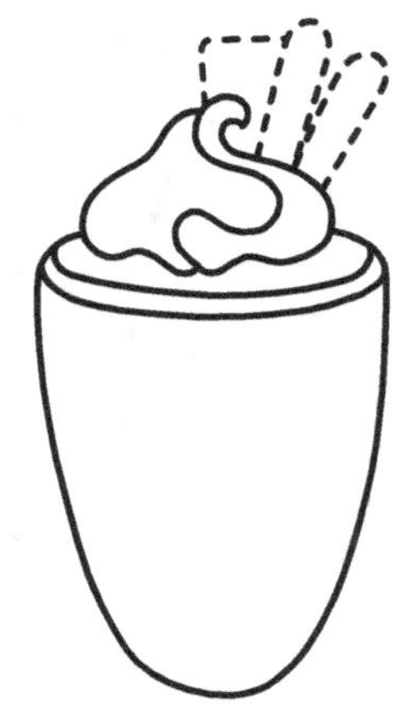

3

Draw the wafers
and chocolate

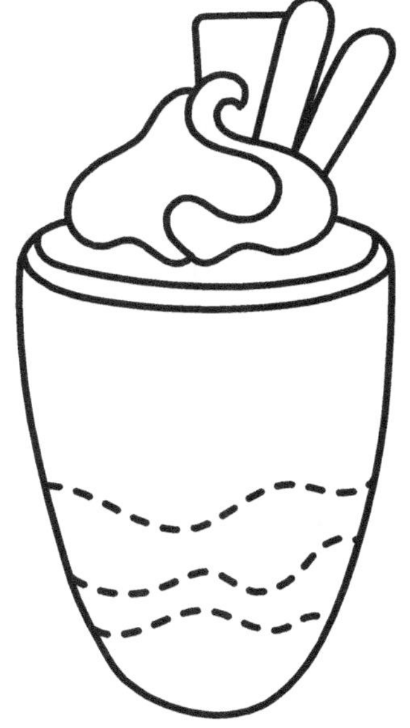

4

Draw the different layers

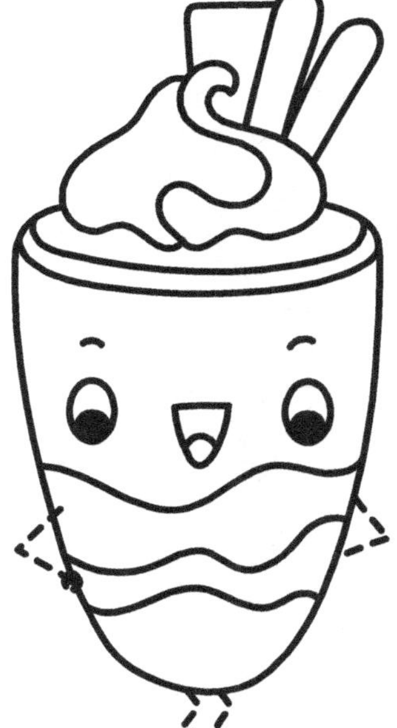

5

Finally, draw cute arms,
legs and face to complete!

PASTRY

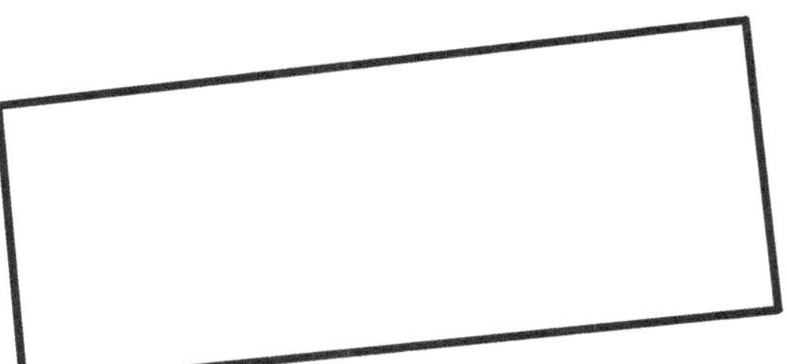

Draw a rectangle

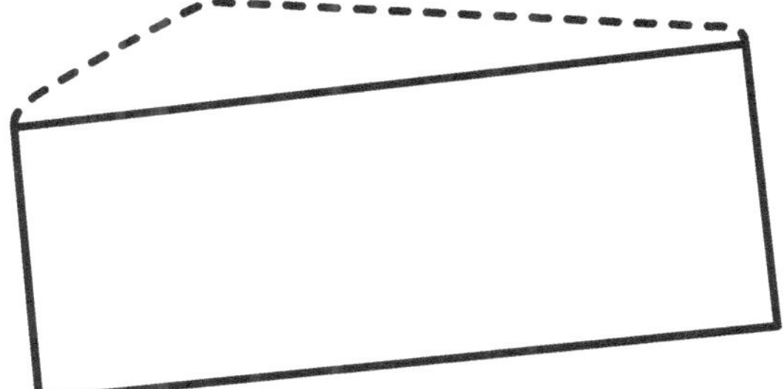

Now make an
adjacent triangle

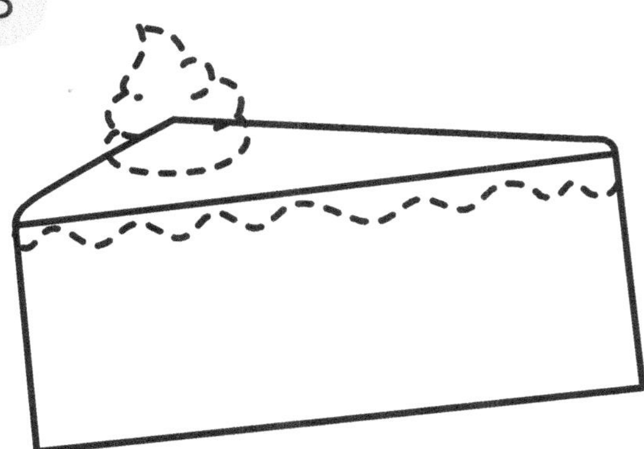

Draw the icing and
cream on top

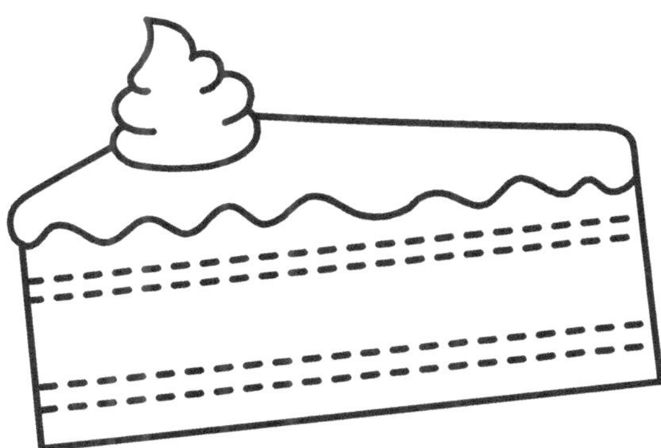

Draw the layers
of the pastry

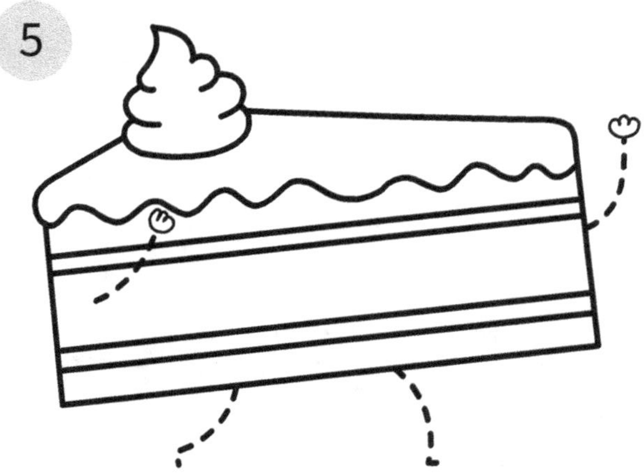

5

Draw cute legs and arms

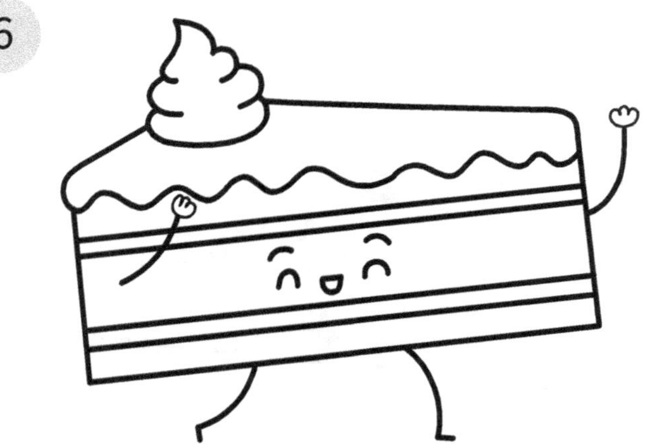

6

Draw a cute face
to finish your pastry!

HOTDOG

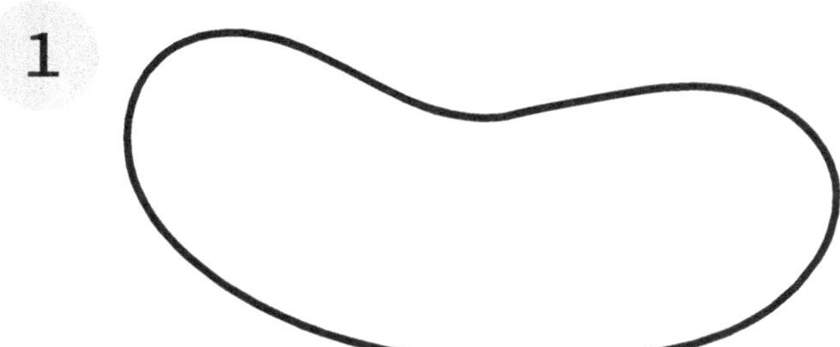

1

Draw a kidney
bean-shaped bread

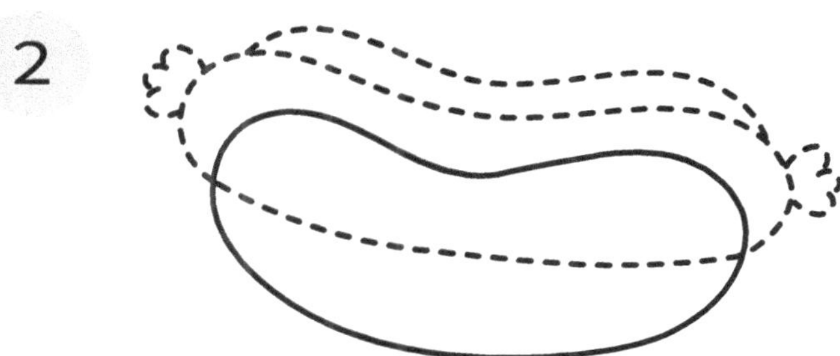

2

Make the sausage and
one more bread

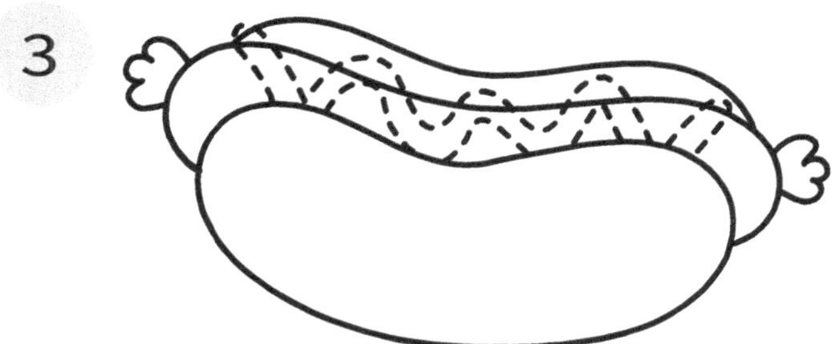

3

Make the yummy
mustard sauce

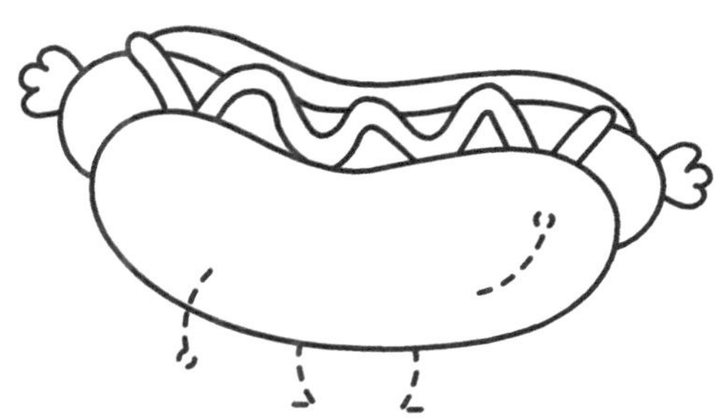

4

Now draw
small legs and arms

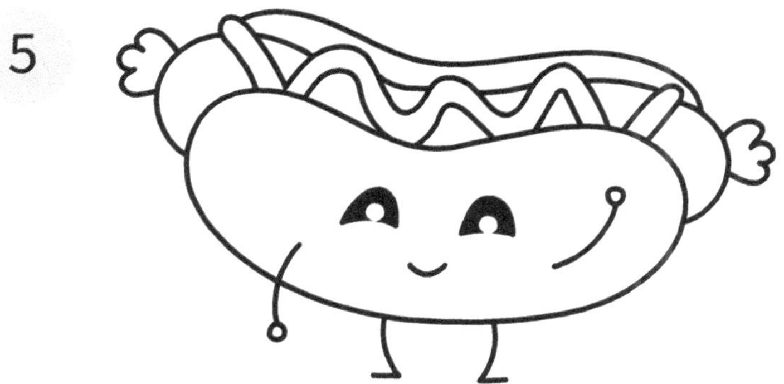

5

Draw an adorable
face to get your hotdog!

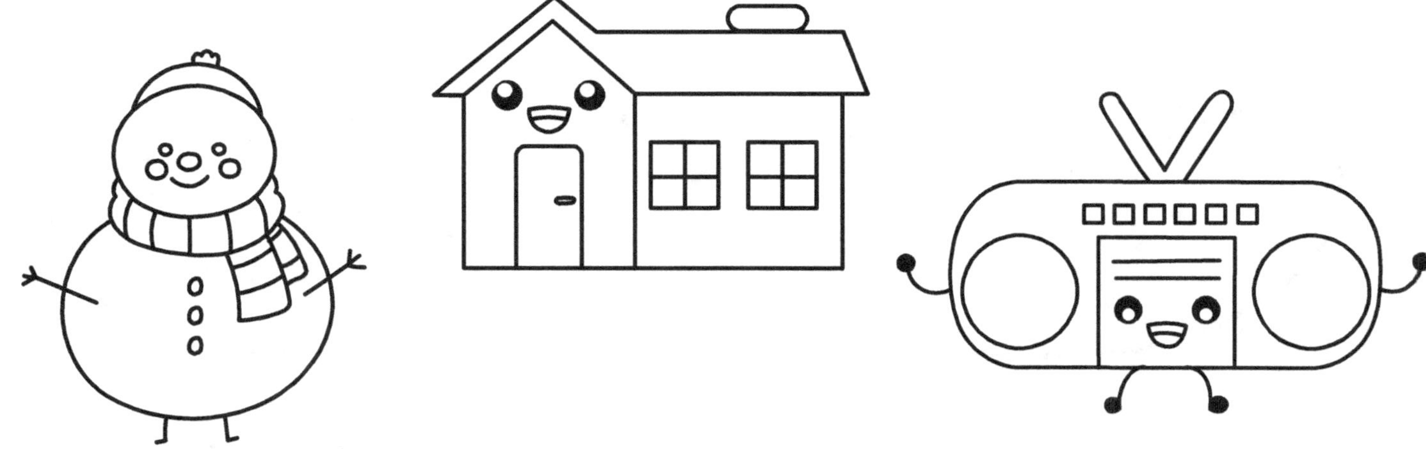

Everyday
Items

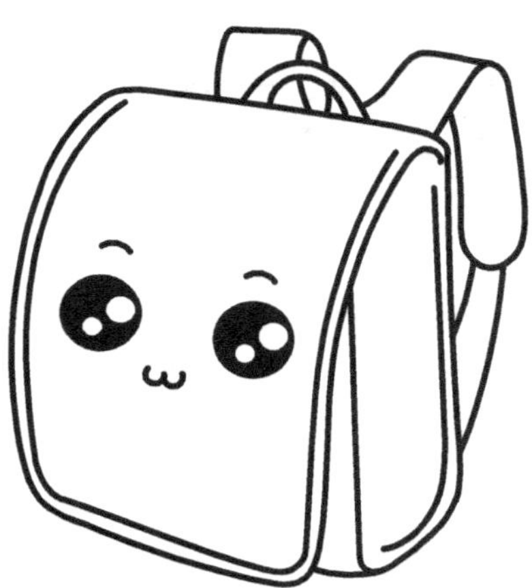

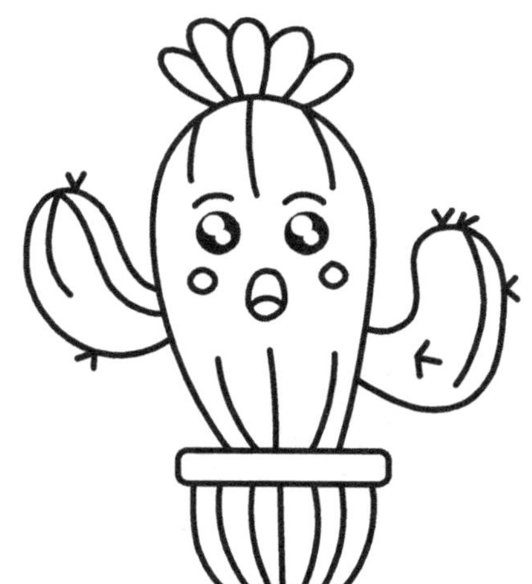

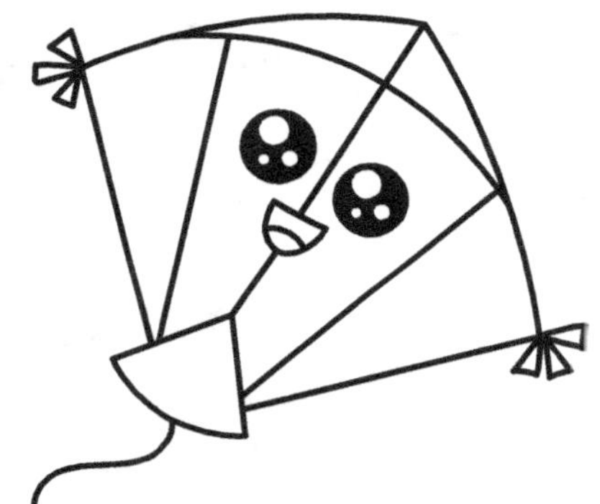

BACKPACK

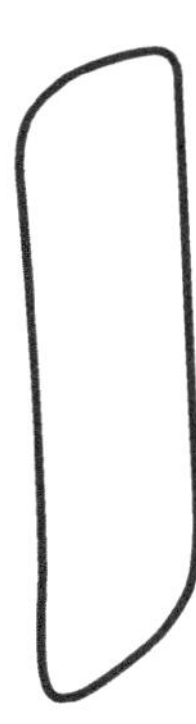

1. Make a rectangle with round edges

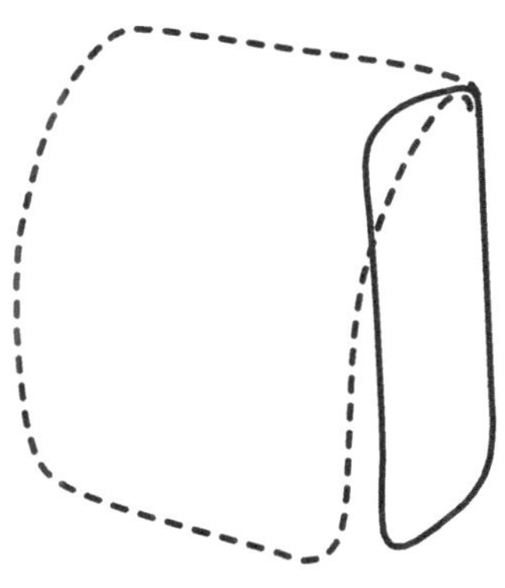

2. Draw the flap

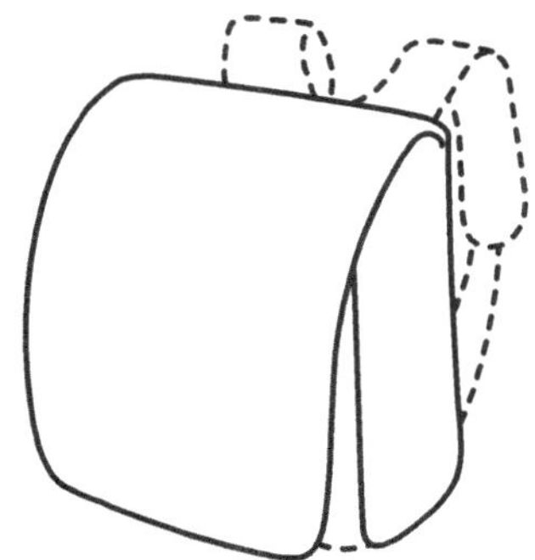

3. Join the two and draw the shoulder straps

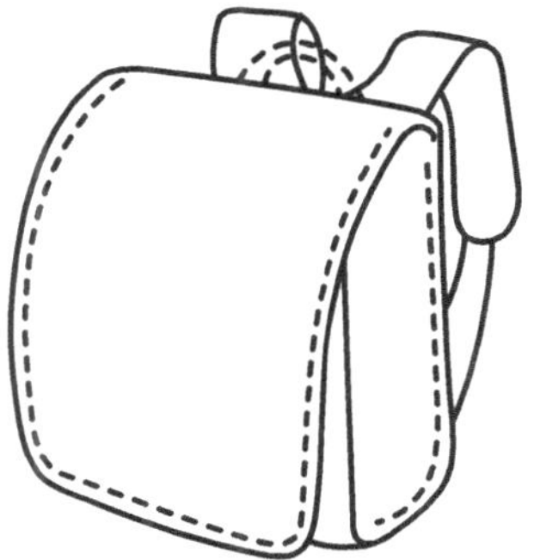

4. Now make the handle and add details

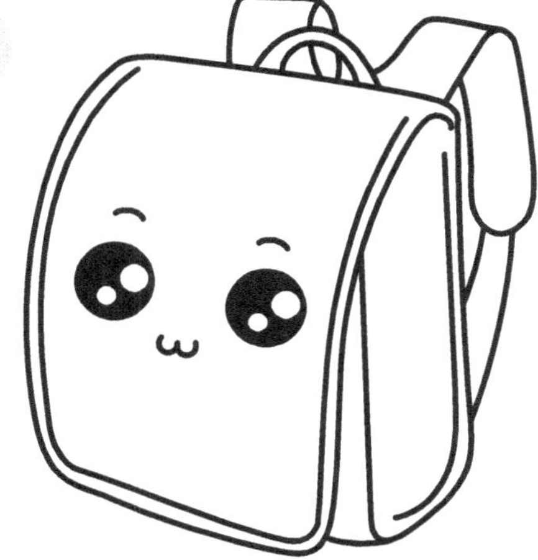

5. Make a cute face for your backpack!

CACTUS

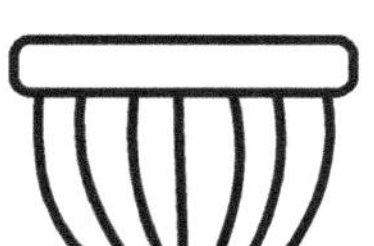

1

Draw a small pot

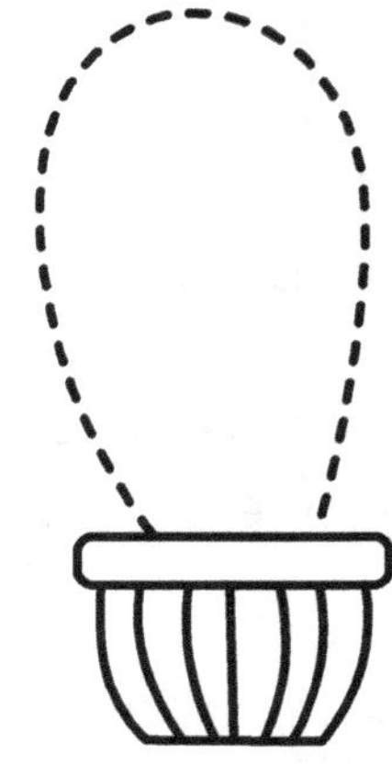

2

Draw the body
of the cactus

3

Make two thick branches

4

Make five cute leaves

5

Now add some details
to your cactus

6

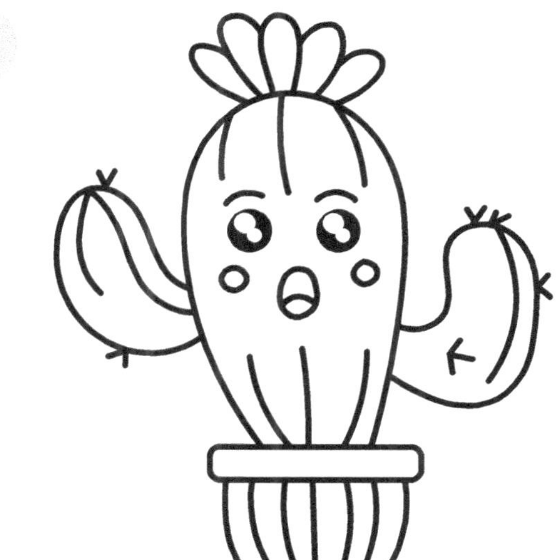

Draw the face and some
thorns to complete it!

KITE

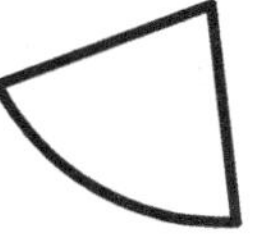

1

Draw a small triangle

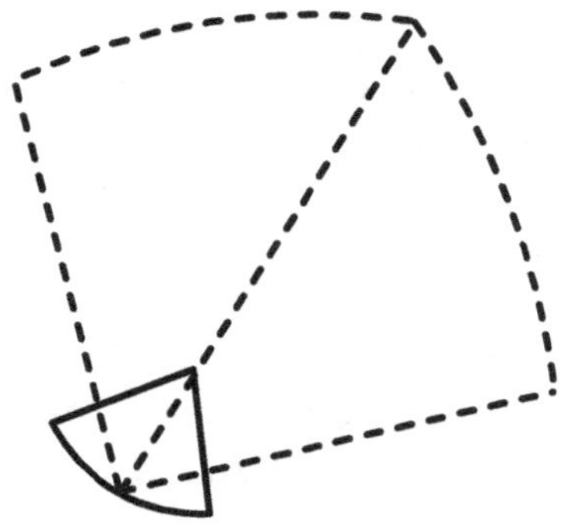

2

Make two more
adjacent triangles

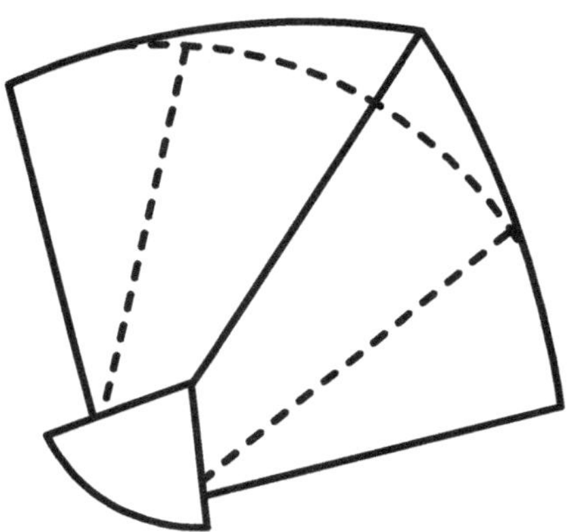

3

Draw some lines
to add details

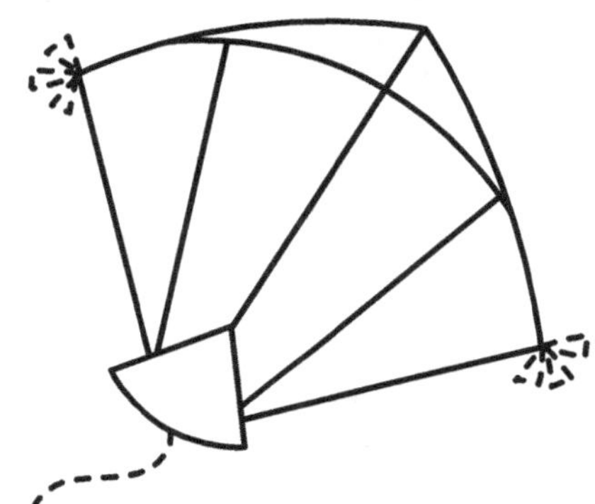

4

Add details on
the side and a tail

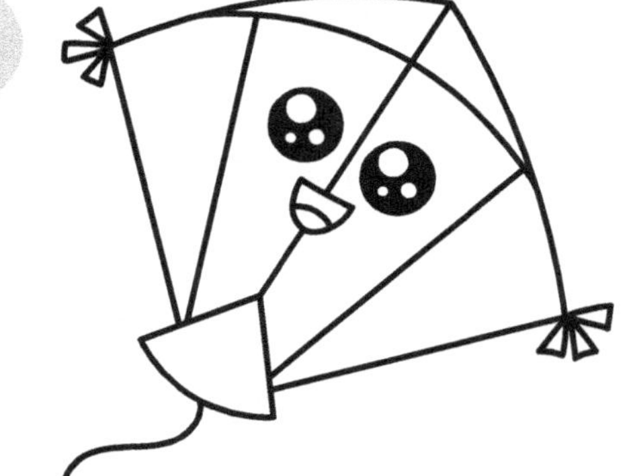

5

Make the face
to complete your kite!

GUITAR

1

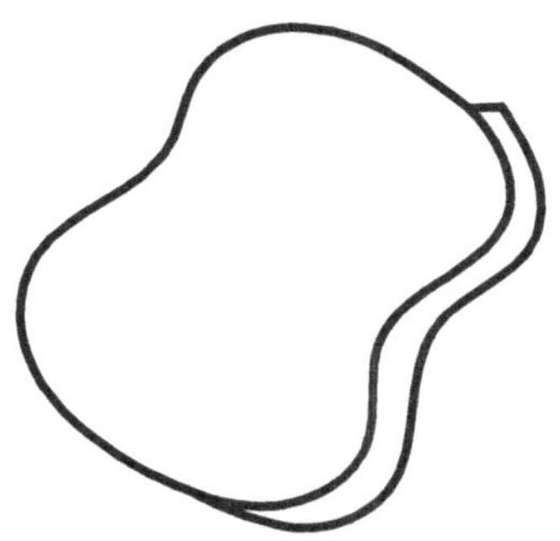

Draw a curvy
shape to begin

2

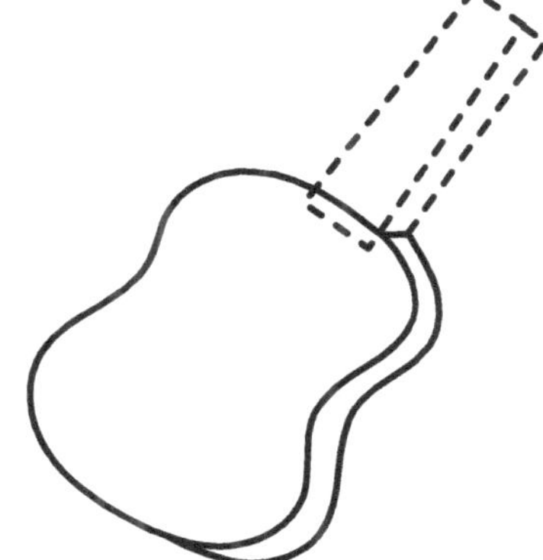

Now make a cuboid

3

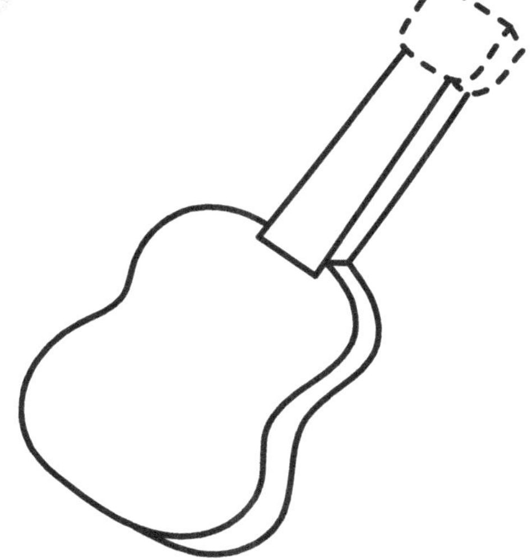

Draw the end of
the guitar

4

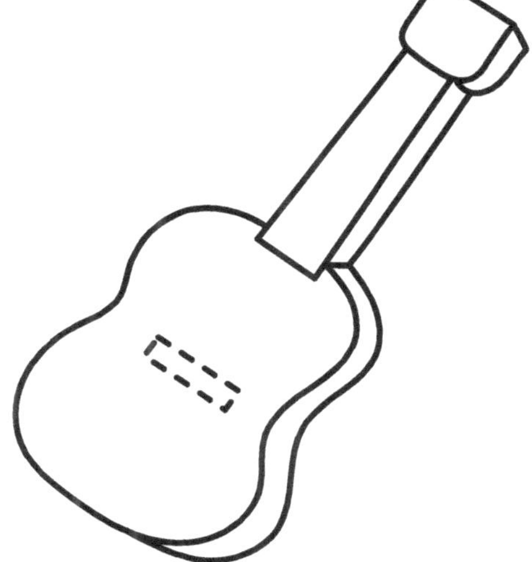

Draw a small rectangle

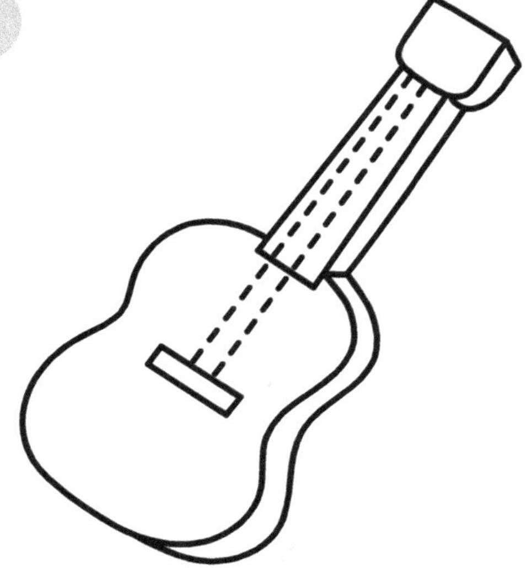

Attach and draw
the strings

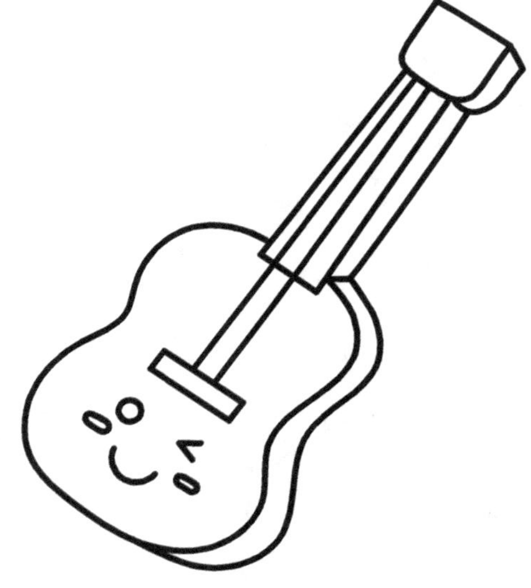

Draw a cute face to
complete your guitar!

RADIO

1

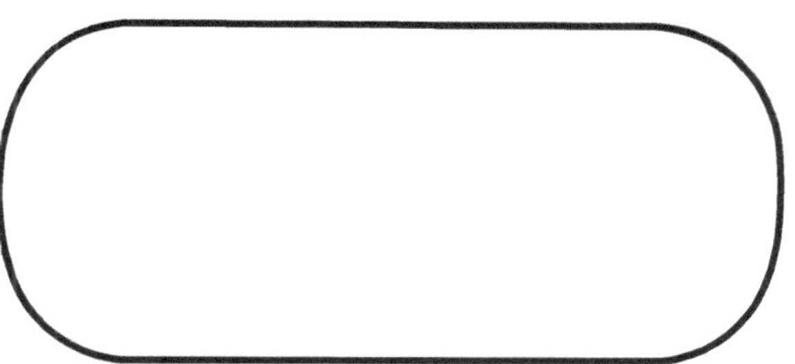

Draw a rectangle with
curved edges

2

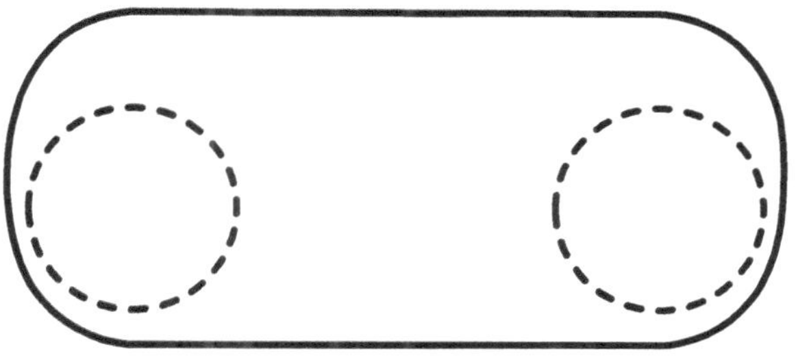

Draw two circles

3

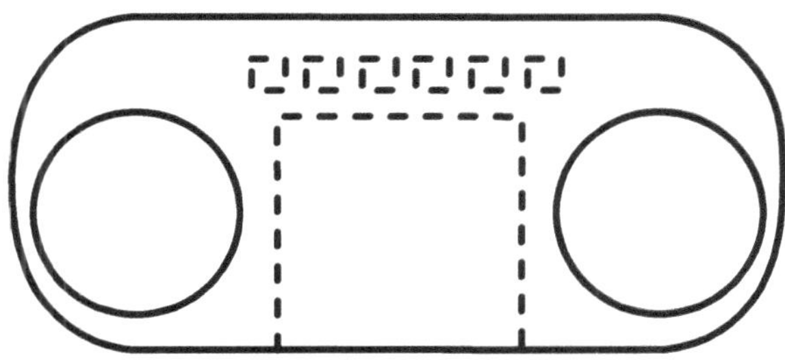

Make a big square and
six small squares

4

Make a bold 'V' on top

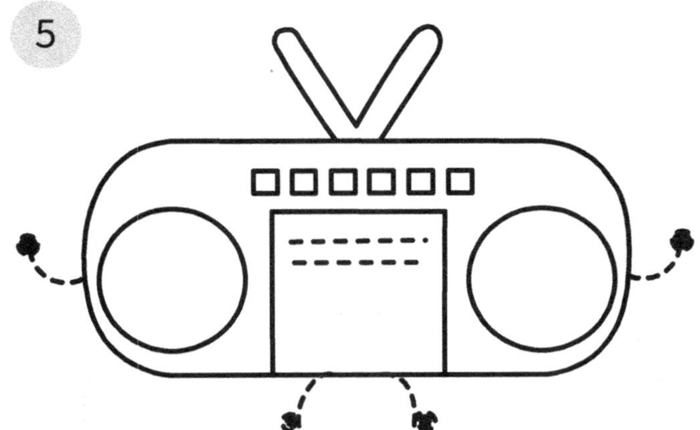

Make cute arms, legs
and add two lines

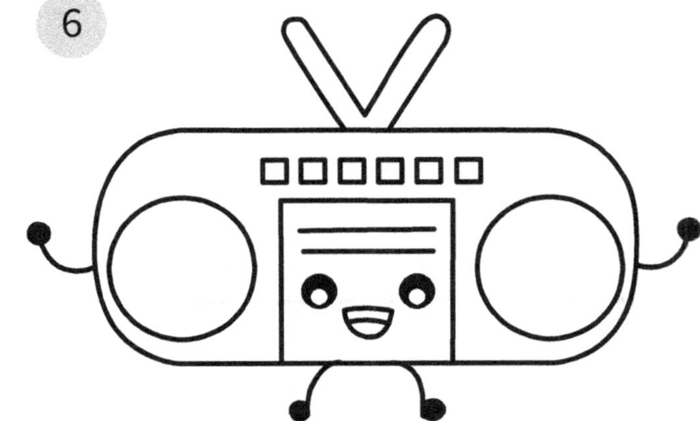

Make the face to
complete your radio!

CASTLE

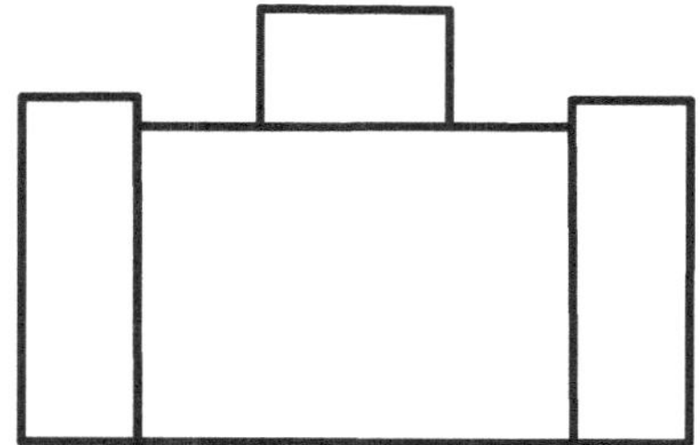

1 Draw four rectangles

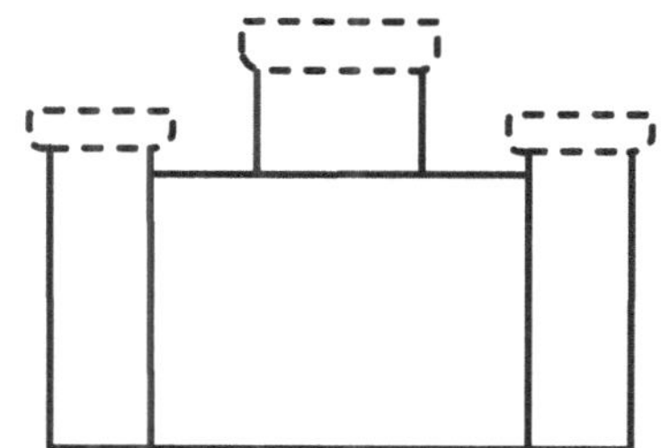

2 Draw three horizontal rectangles

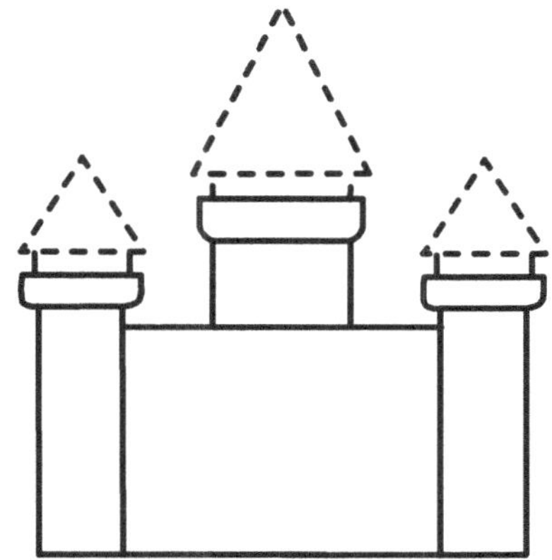

3 Now draw one big triangle and two small triangles

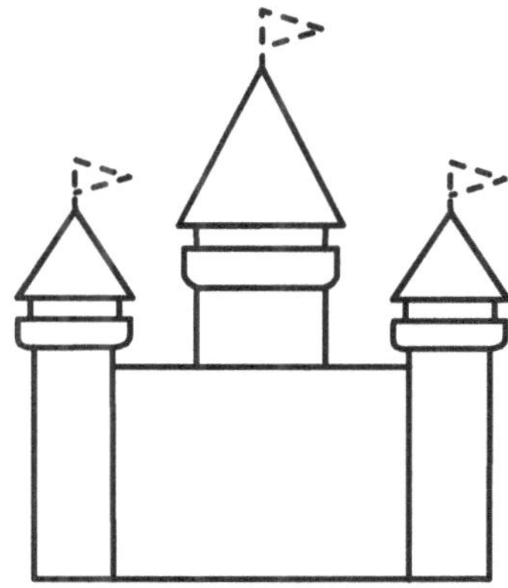

4 Draw three flags

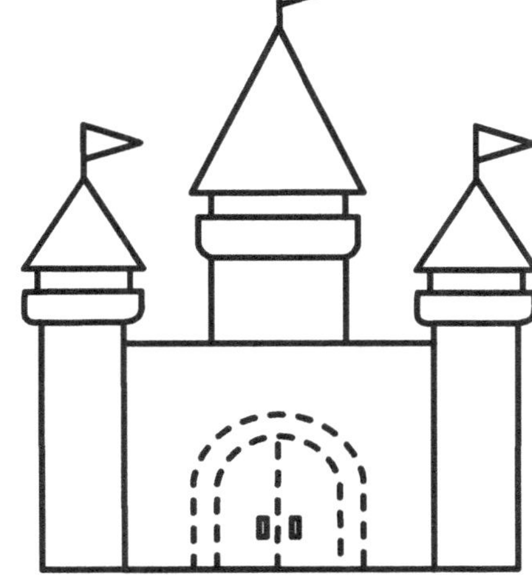

5 Draw the gates of the castle to complete it!

SNOWMAN

1

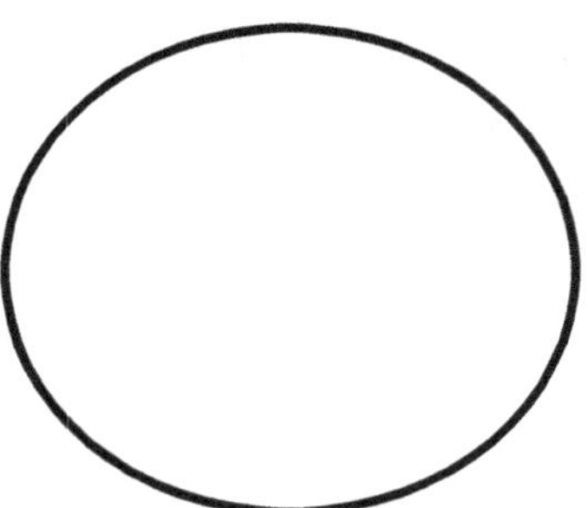

Draw a big oval

2

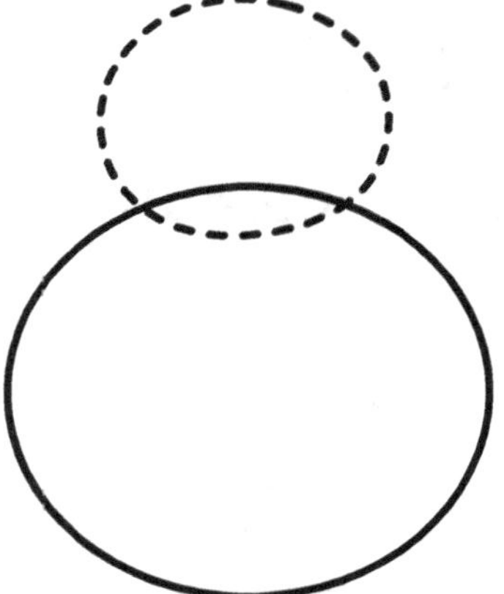

Draw a small
oval above it

3

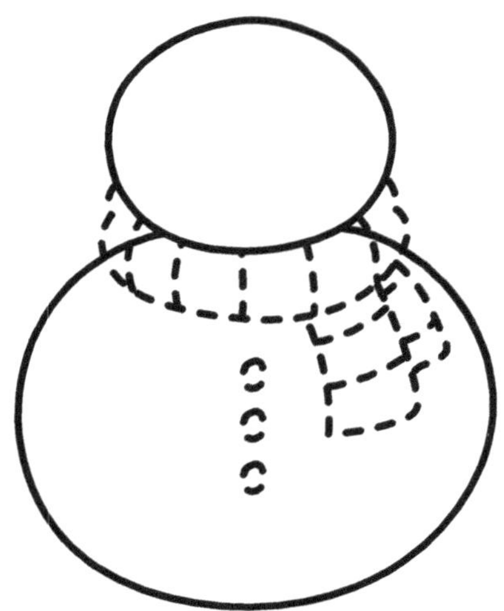

Draw the muffler
and buttons

4

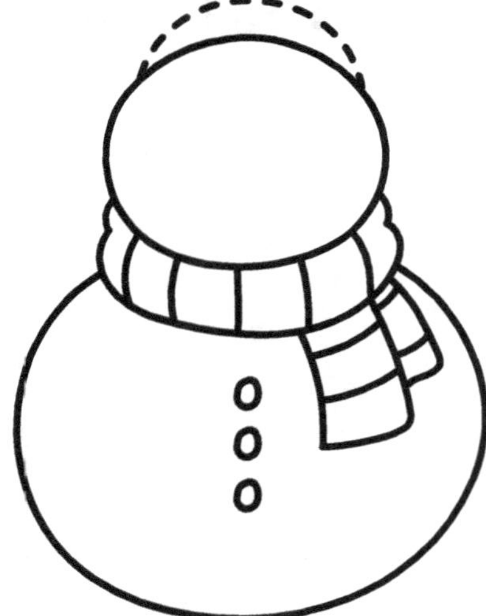

Make a hat
for your snowman

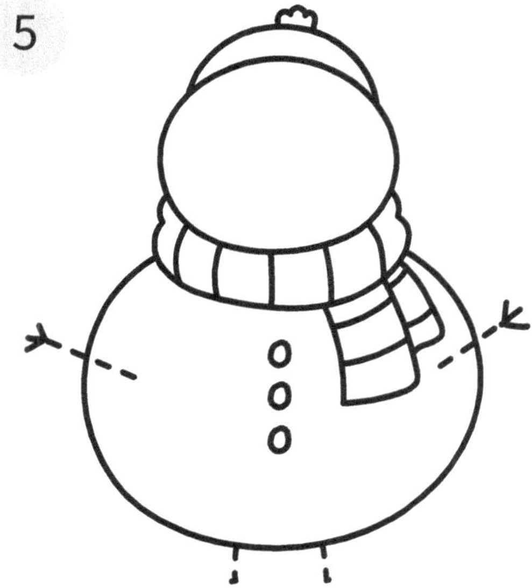

5

Draw the arms and legs

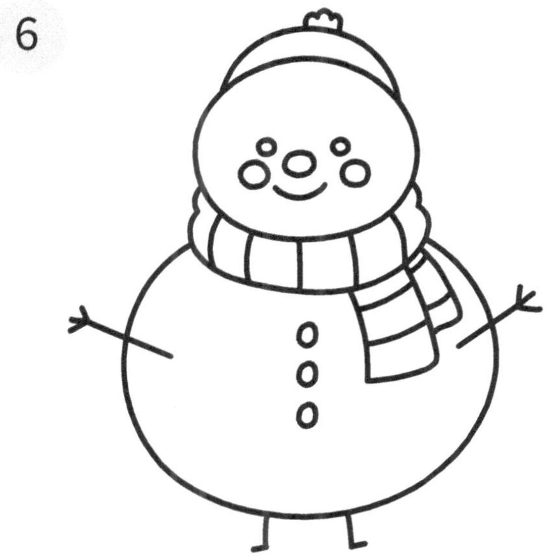

6

Make a cute face to
complete your snowman!

HOUSE

1

Begin by drawing
a rectangle

2

Draw a square with
a triangle on top

3

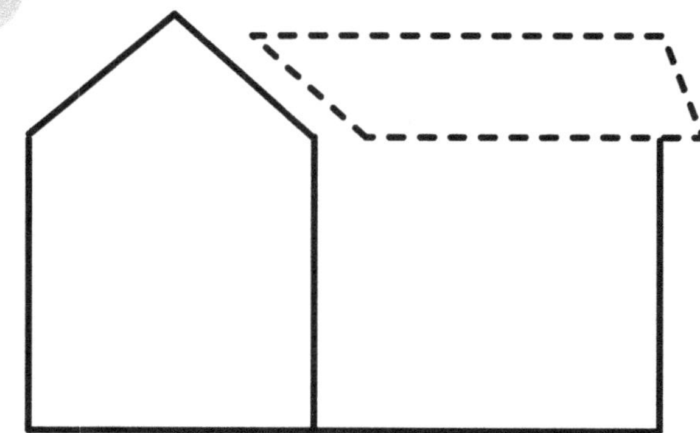

Draw one more rectangle

4

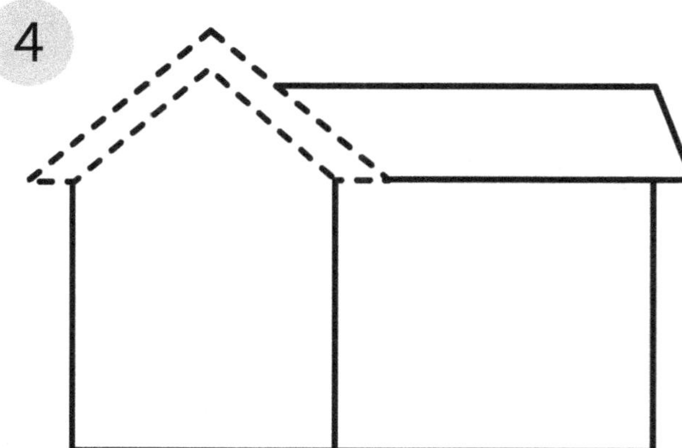

Now draw an inverted 'V'

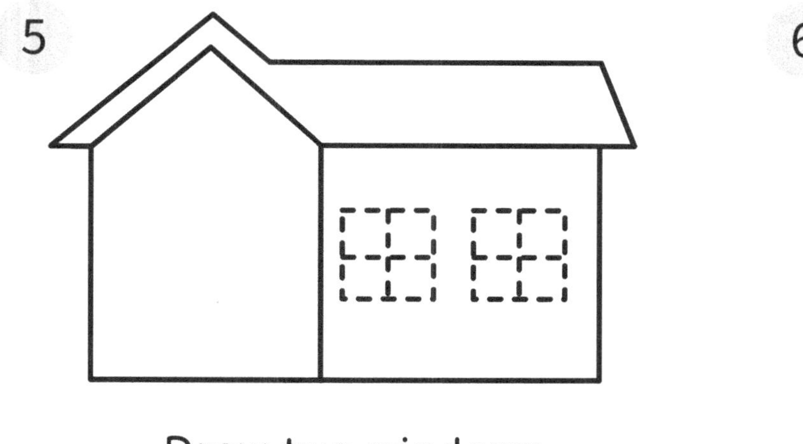

5 Draw two windows

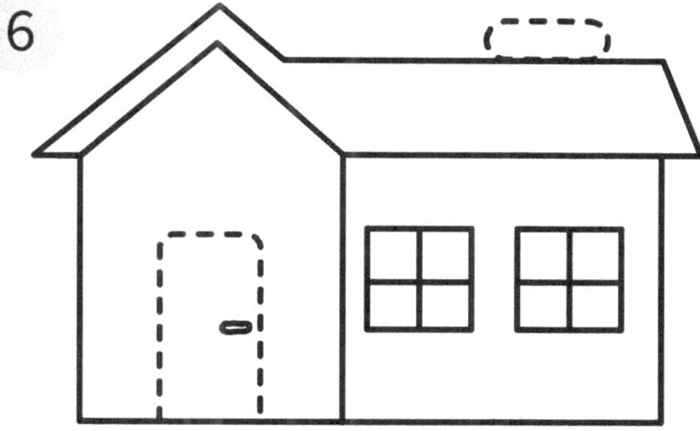

6 Draw the chimney
and the door

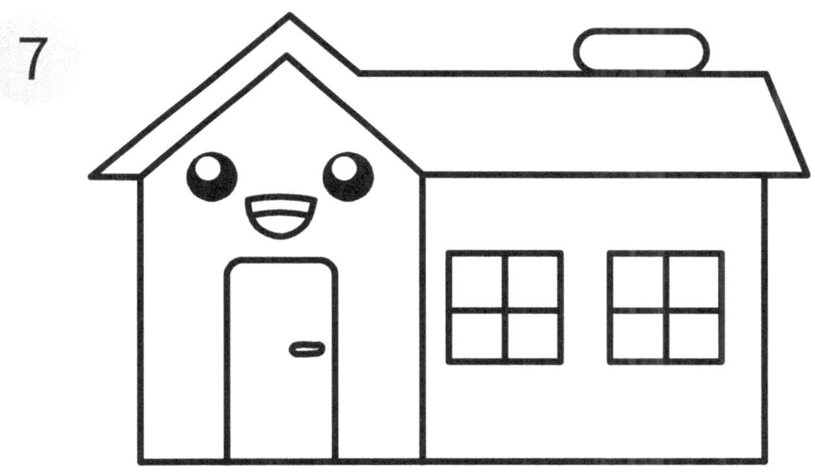

7 Draw the face to finish your house!

FLOWER

1

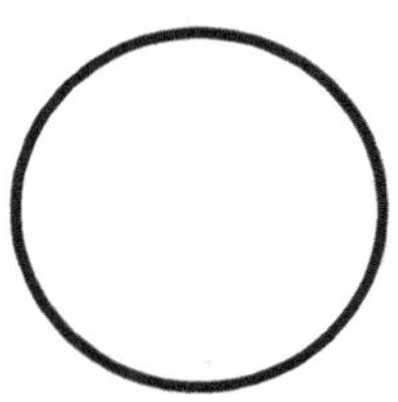

Start by drawing a circle

2

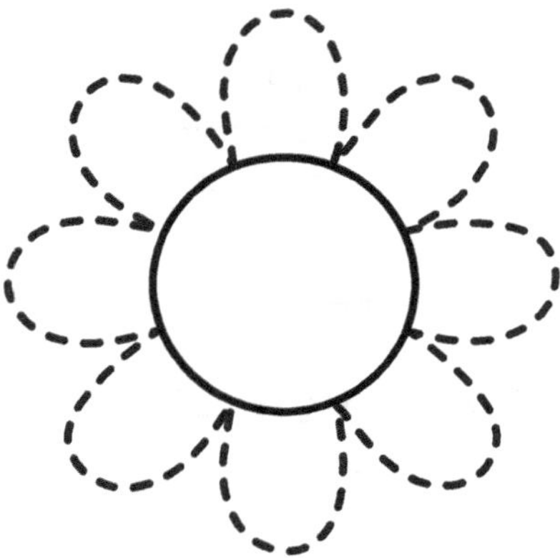

Draw eight
oval-shaped petals

3

Draw a pattern
inside the petals

4

Draw twelve
heart-shaped petals

5

Make the face to
complete your flower!

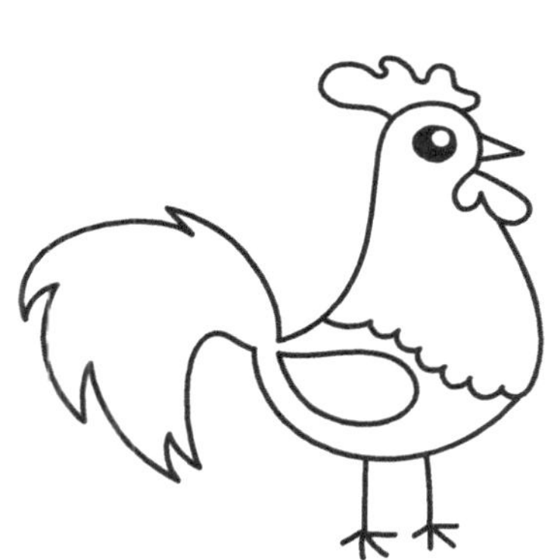
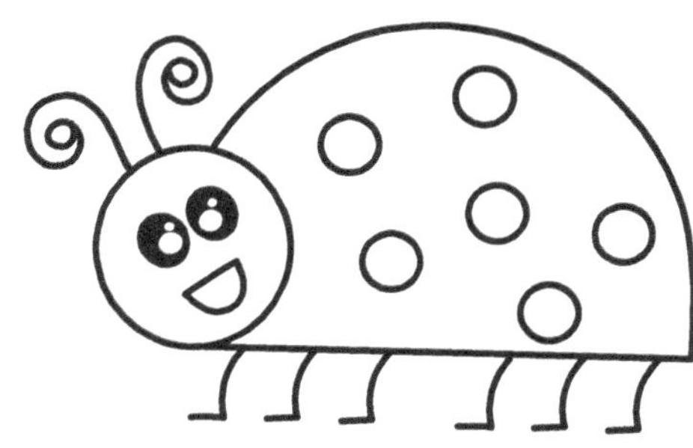
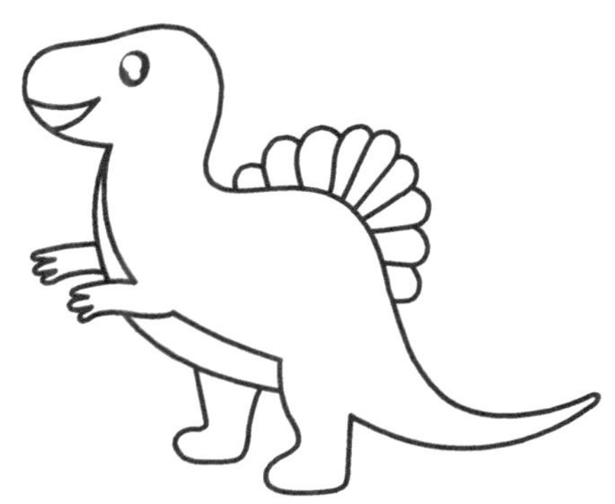

Cute
Animals

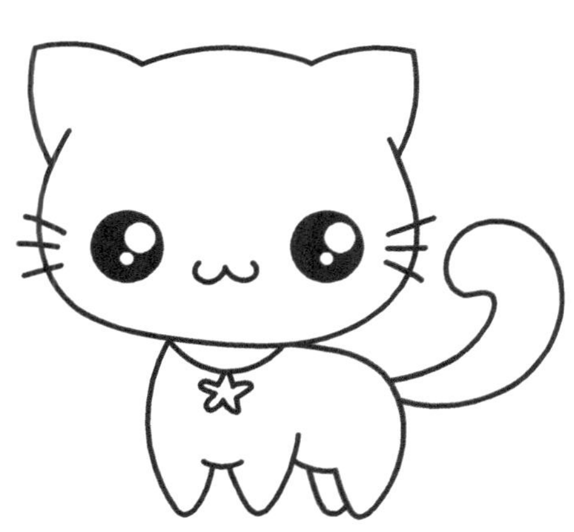
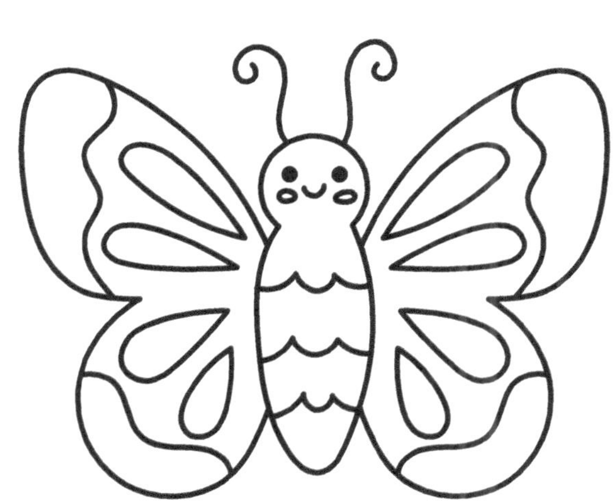
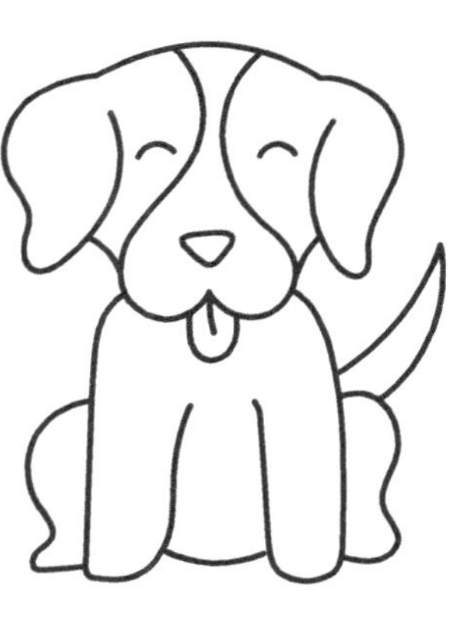

HEN

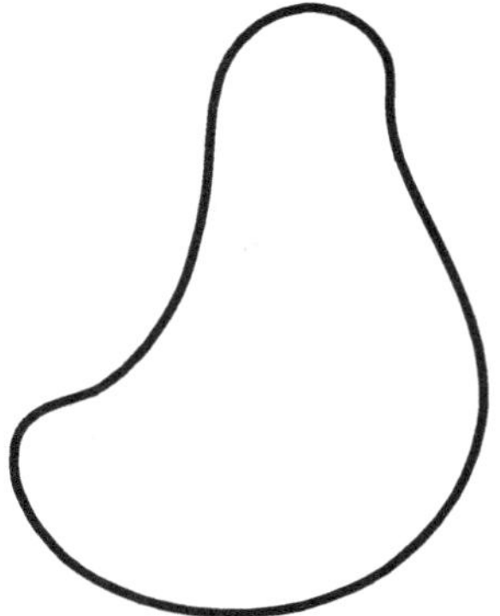

Draw an oval with one narrow end

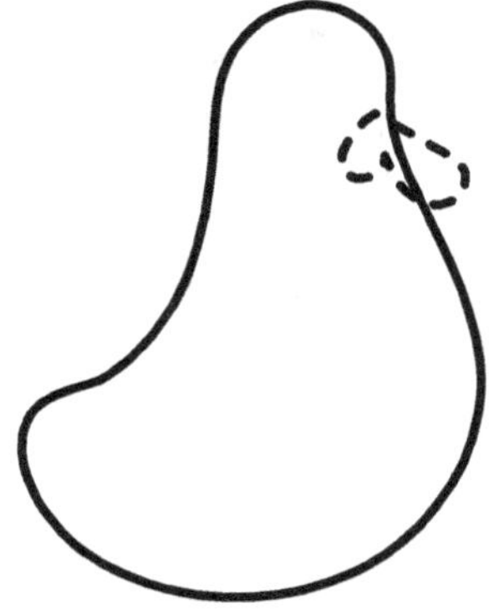

Now draw an inverted heart

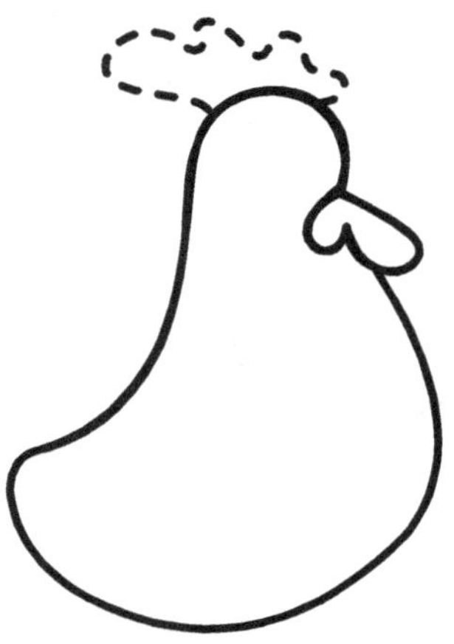

Draw the hen's comb

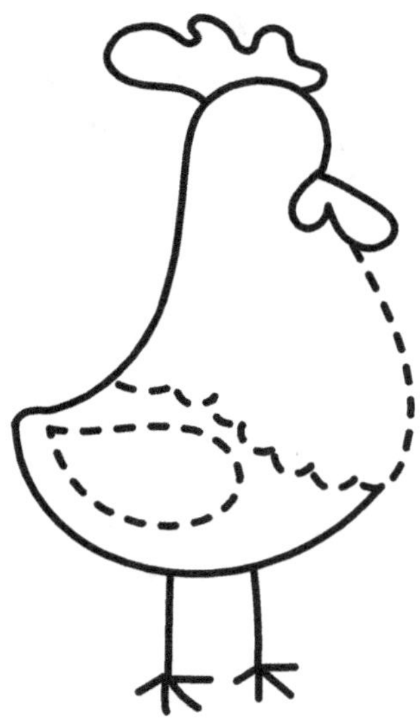

Draw a drop-shaped feather and add detail

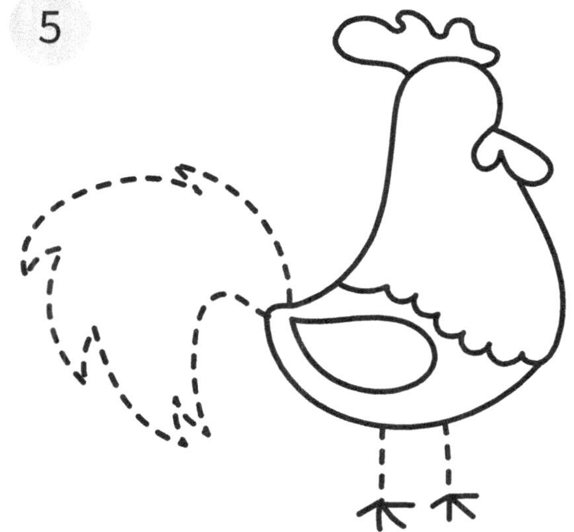

Draw the tail and legs

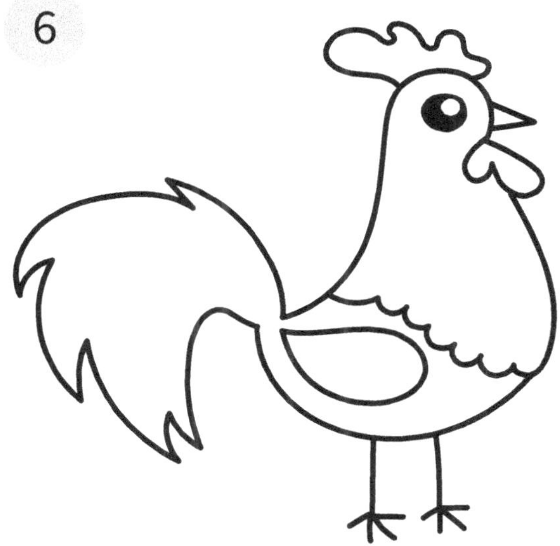

Draw the eyes and beak
to complete the hen!

DINOSAUR

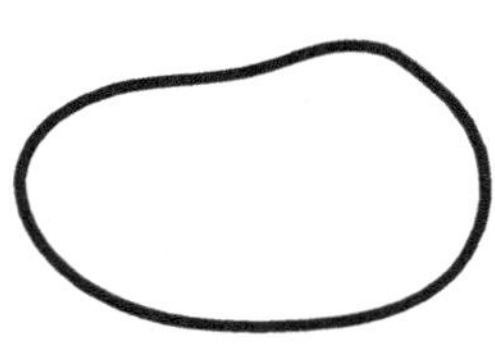

Draw a small oval to start

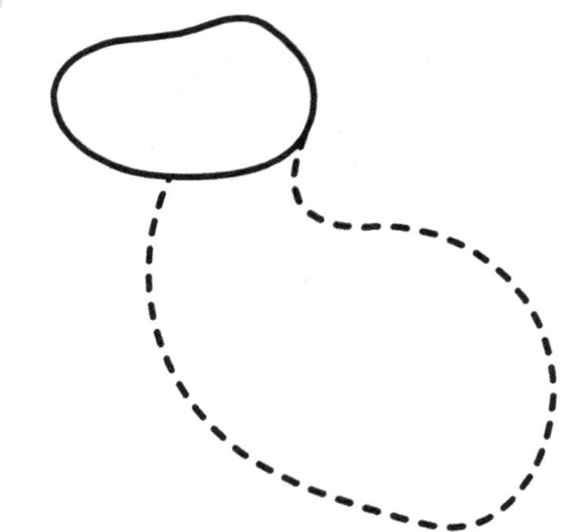

Draw a bigger oval for the body

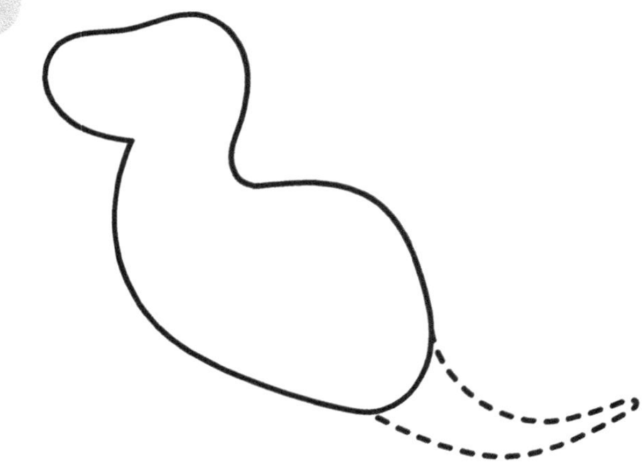

Make a long tail

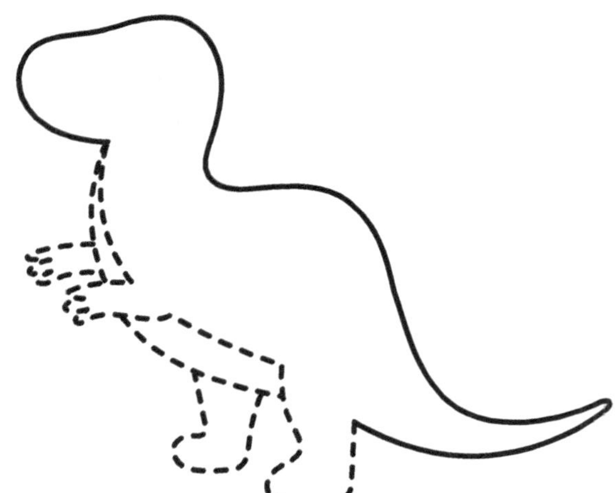

Draw four cute limbs

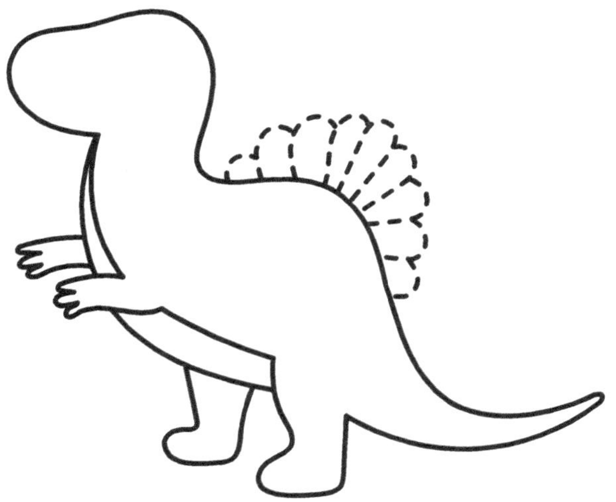

Now make the scales

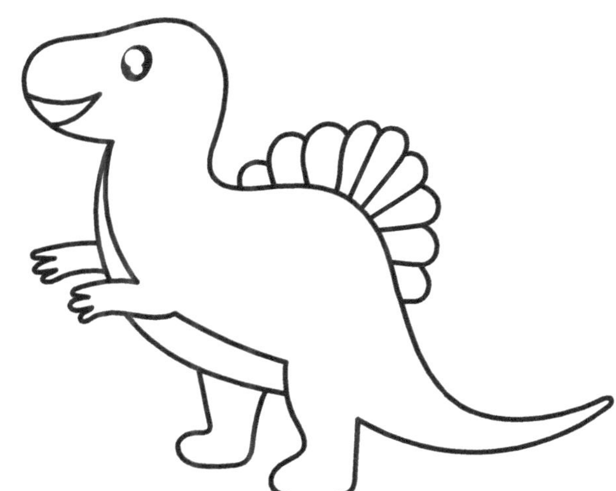

Draw the face
to complete!

BUTTERFLY

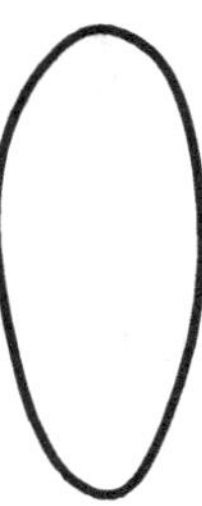

Draw an elongated oval

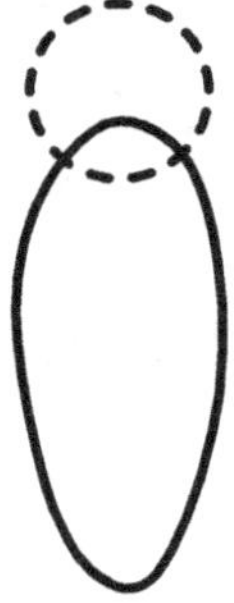

Draw a circle
for the head

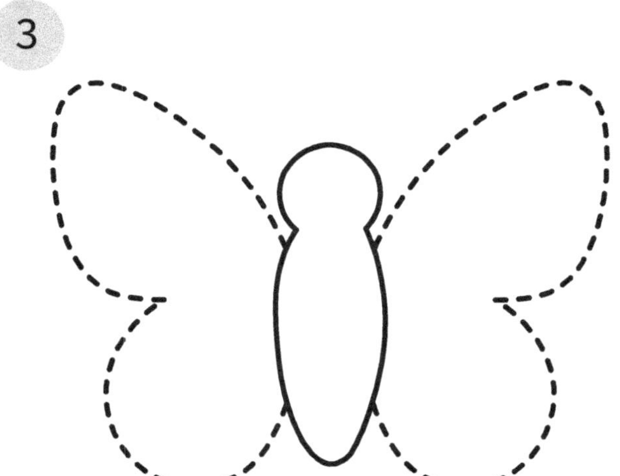

Draw two
symmetrical wings

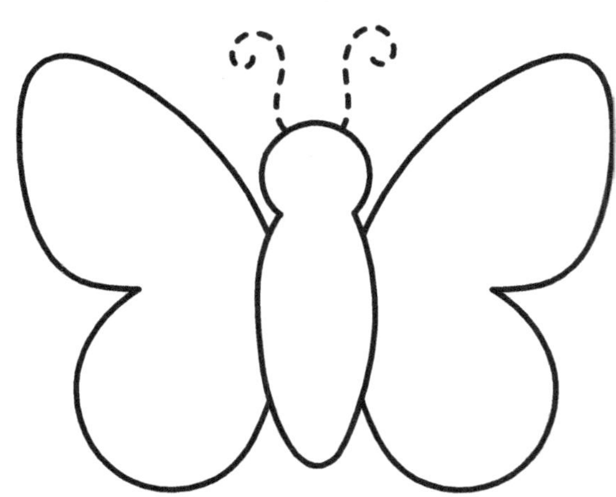

Now make curly antennas

5

Add details to decorate

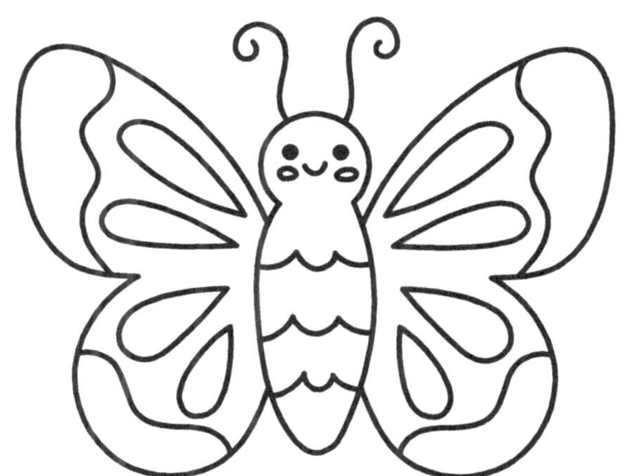

6

Make a cute face to
complete your butterfly!

CAT

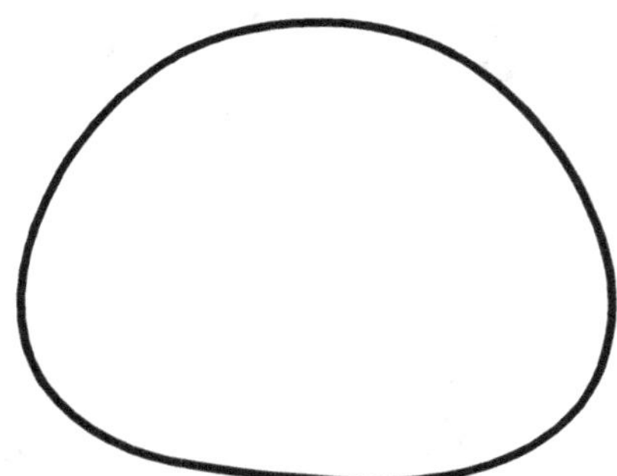

1

Start by drawing a
circular head

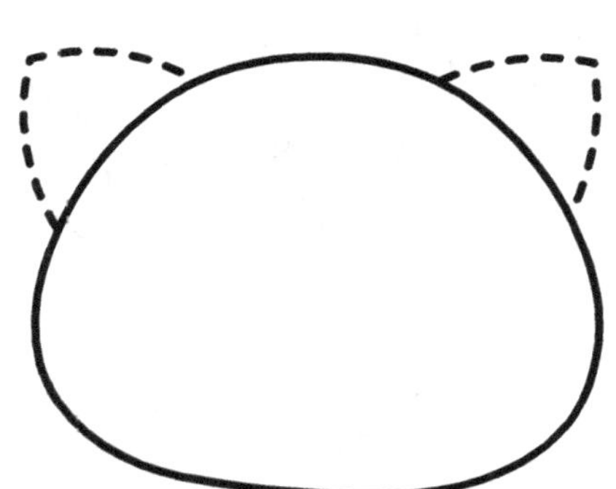

2

Draw two triangular ears

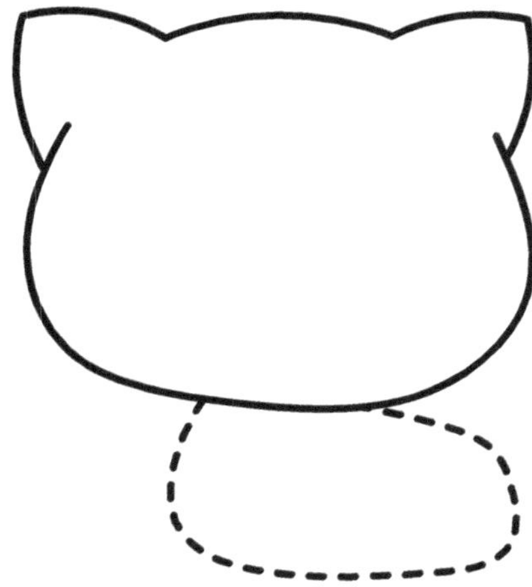

3

Draw an oval for the body

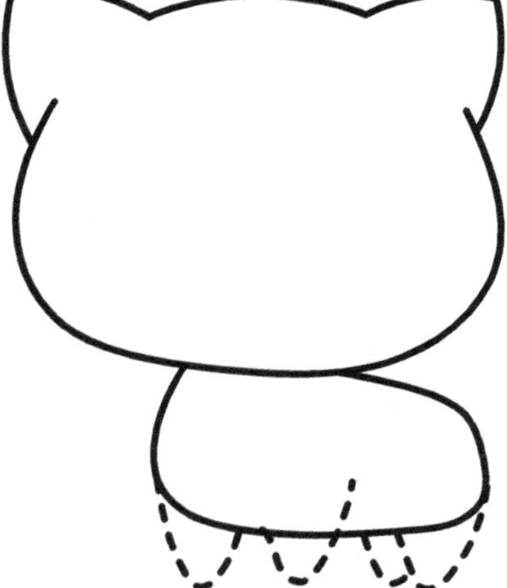

4

Make four cute legs

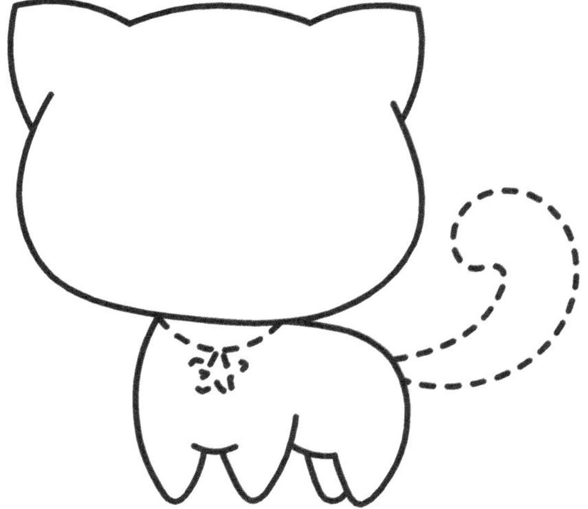

Make a fluffy
tail and the collar

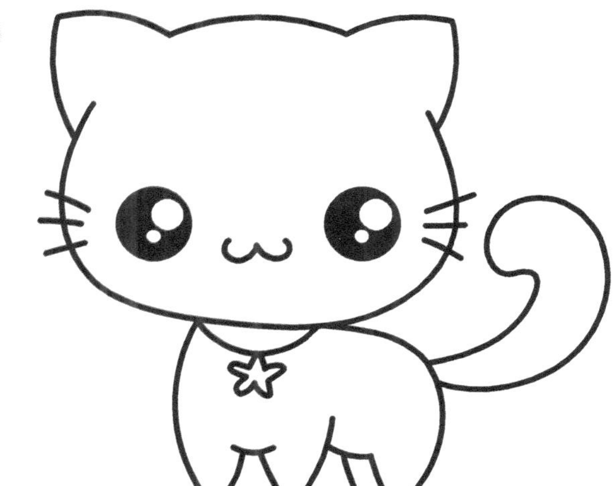

Draw the face and
whiskers to complete
your kitty!

LADY BUG

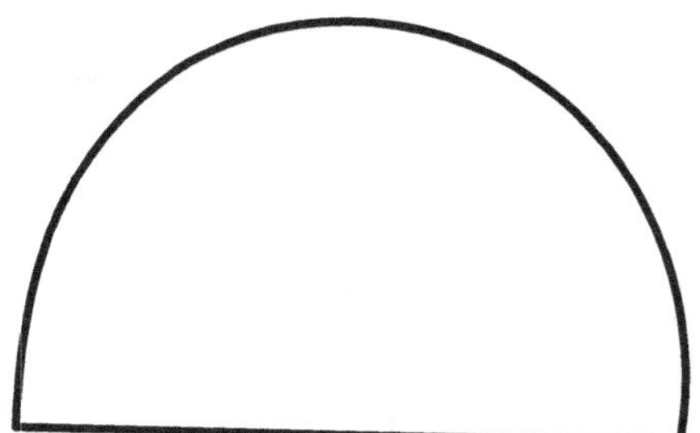

Draw a semi circle

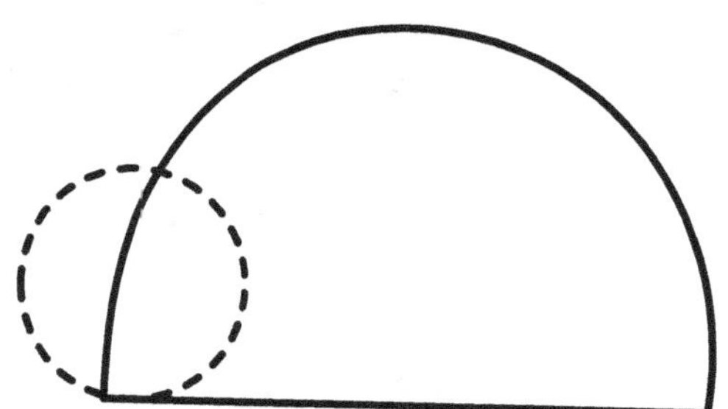

Make a circle
for the head

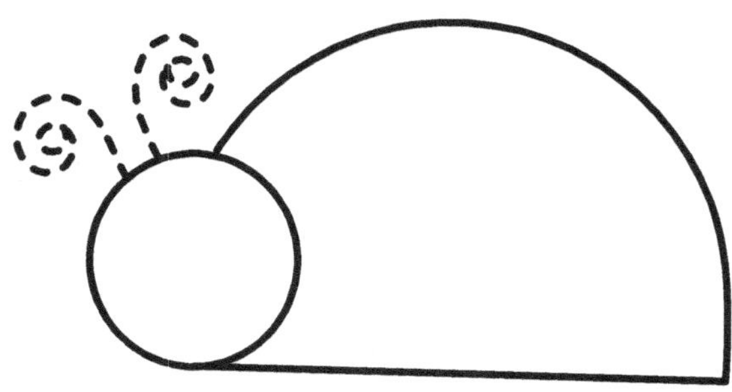

Draw two curly antennas

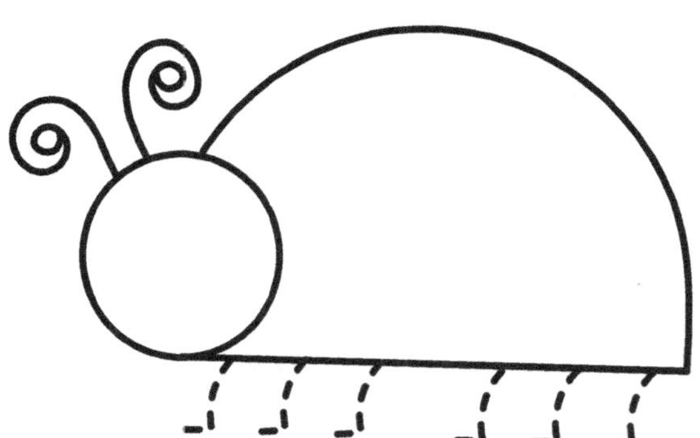

Make six tiny legs

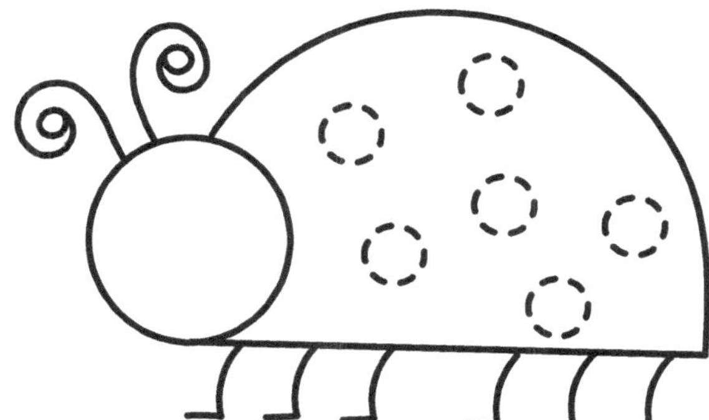

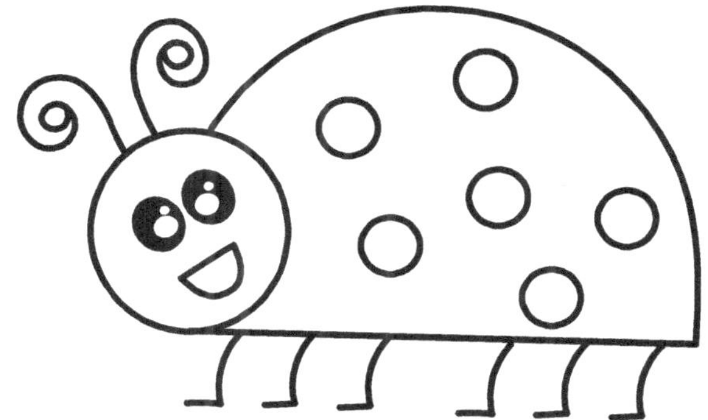

Add details by drawing
small circles

Draw the face to
complete the lady bug!

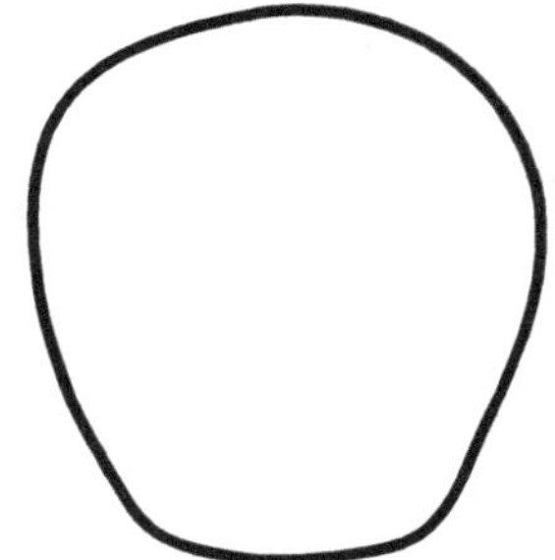

1

Start by drawing
an oval face

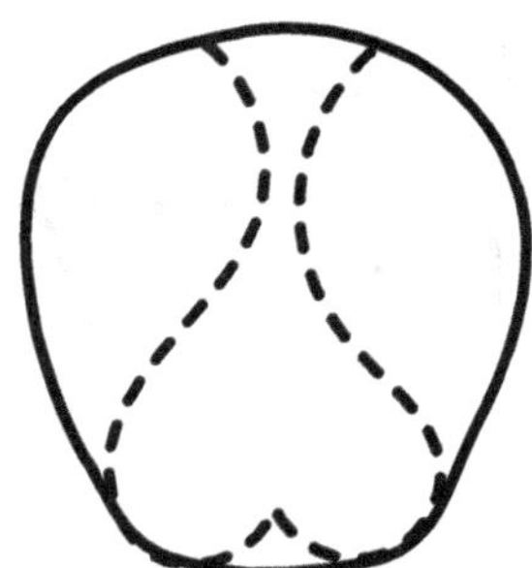

2

Draw an inverted
heart-shaped

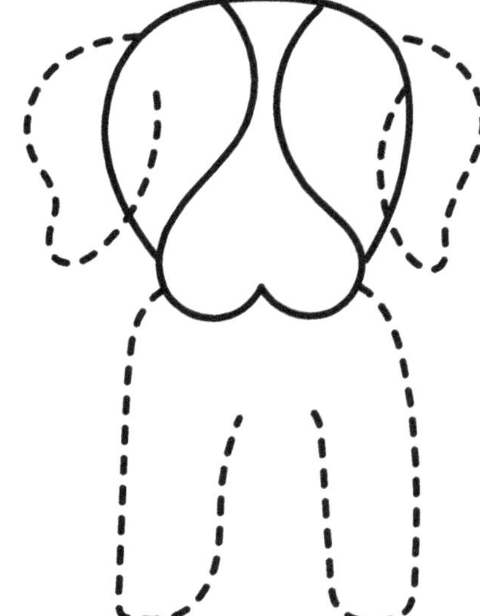

3

Make two flappy ears
and two long legs

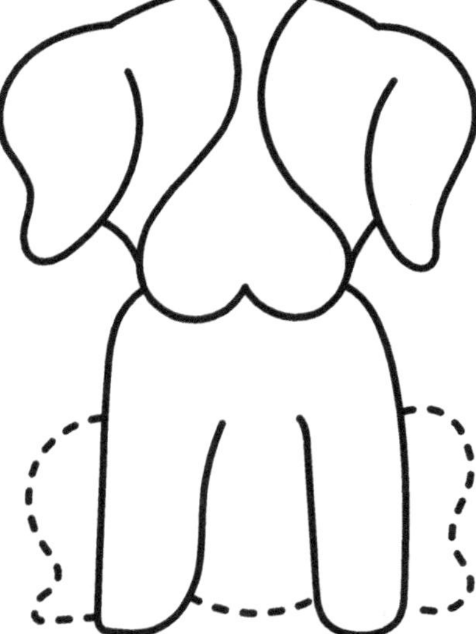

4

Join them and
draw hind legs

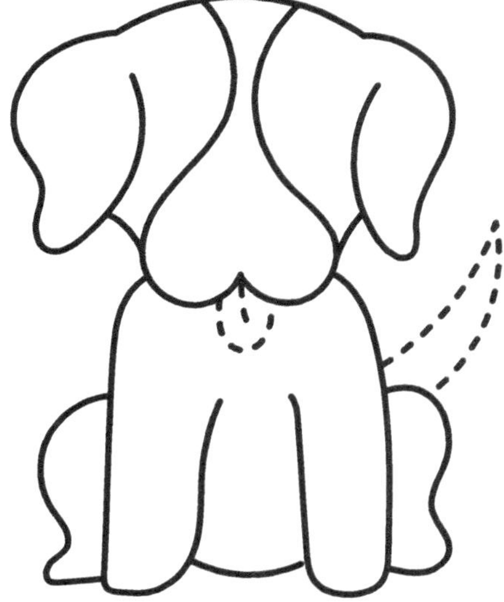

5

Draw a long tail
and the tongue

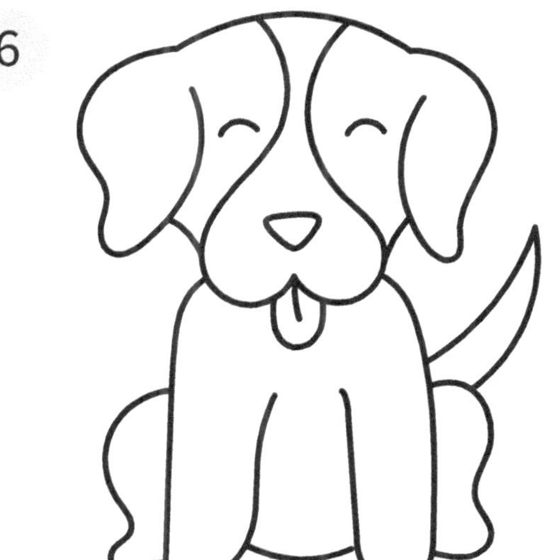

6

Draw the face
to complete your dog!

PENGUIN

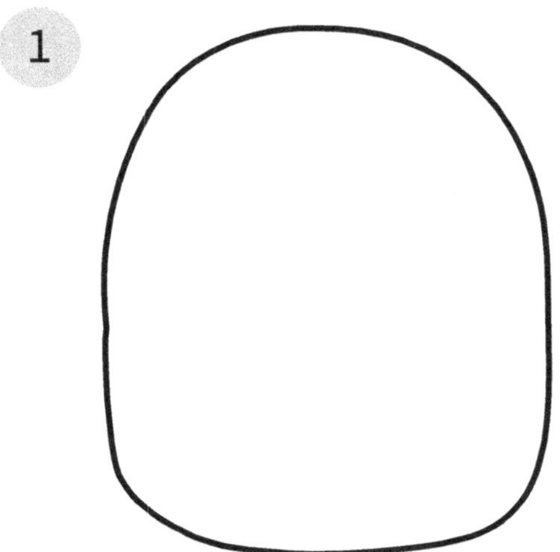

Start with making the
body of the penguin

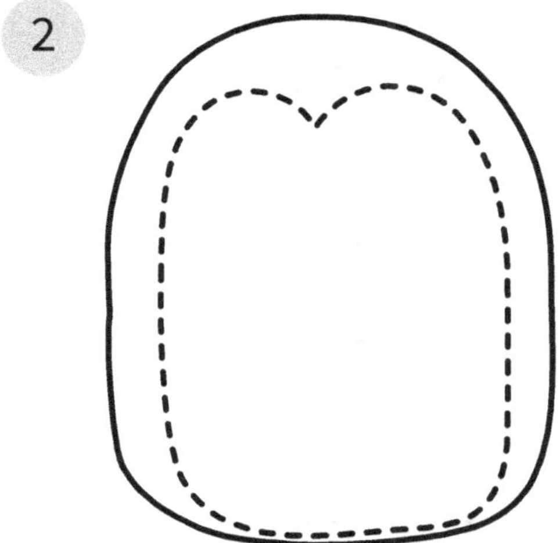

Draw the outline
of the fur

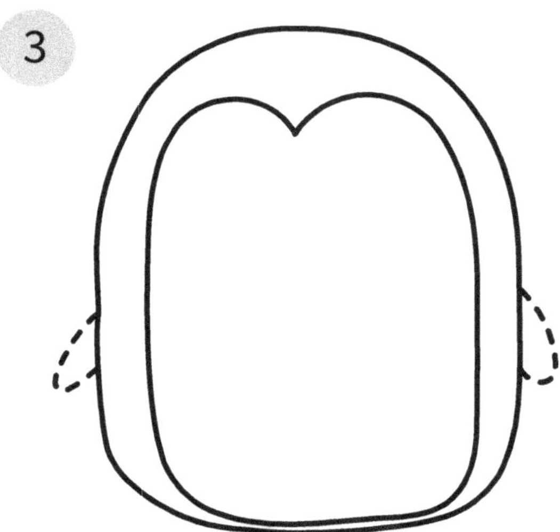

Draw two cute, little hands

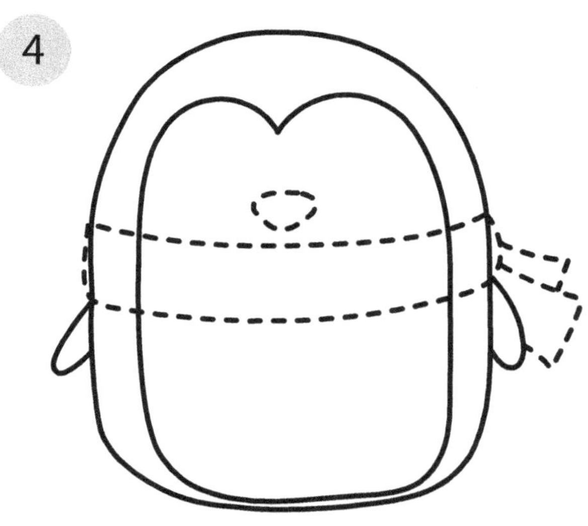

Draw the muffler
and a cute little nose

5

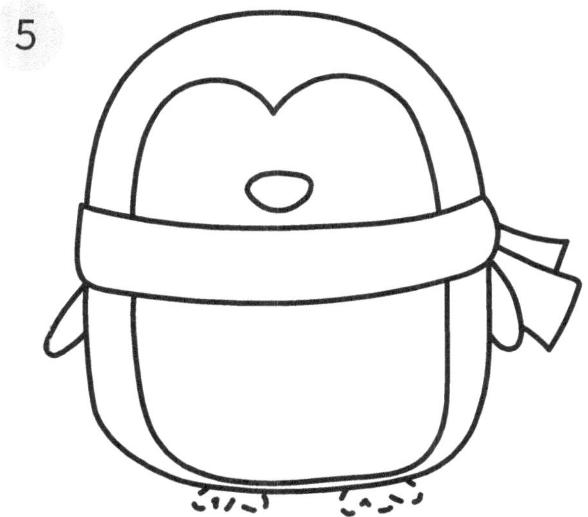

Draw two small feet

6

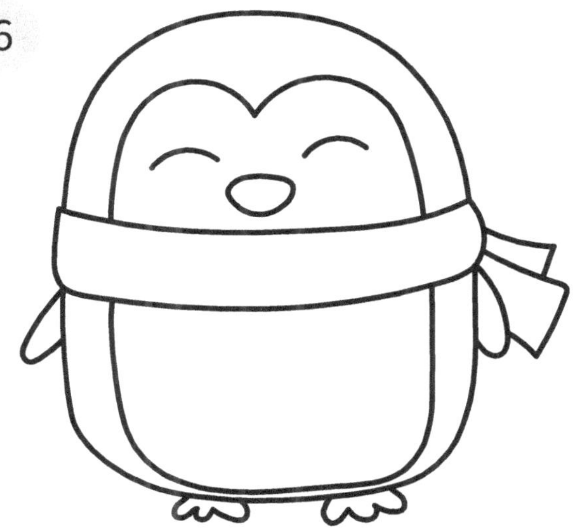

Draw the eyes to
complete your penguin!

TURTLE

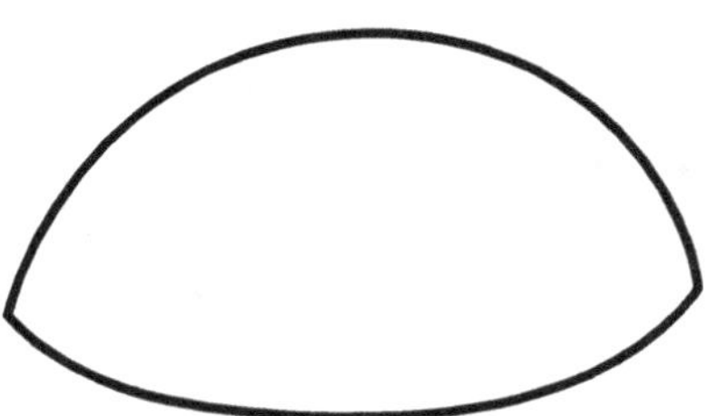

Start by drawing the shell

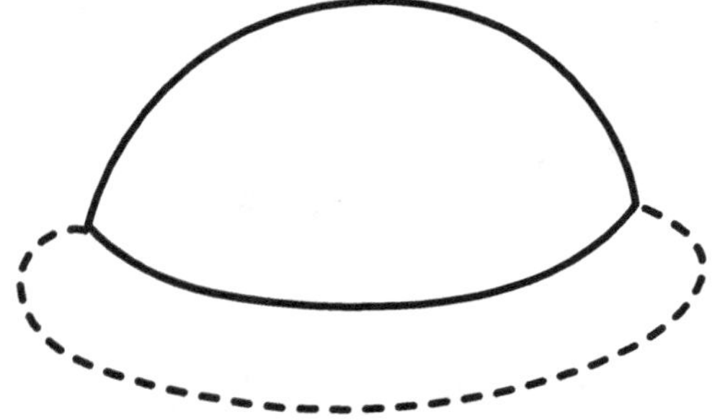

Draw a thick border
of the shell

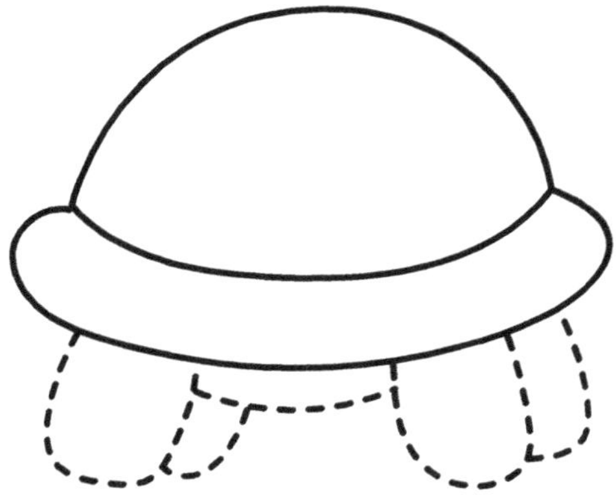

Draw four cute,
round legs

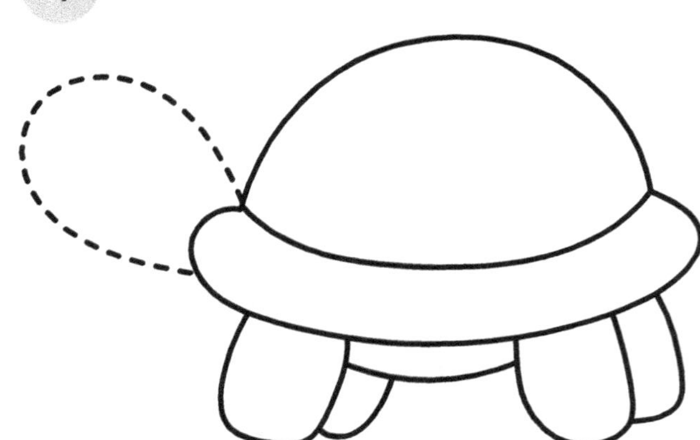

Draw the head
of the turtle

5

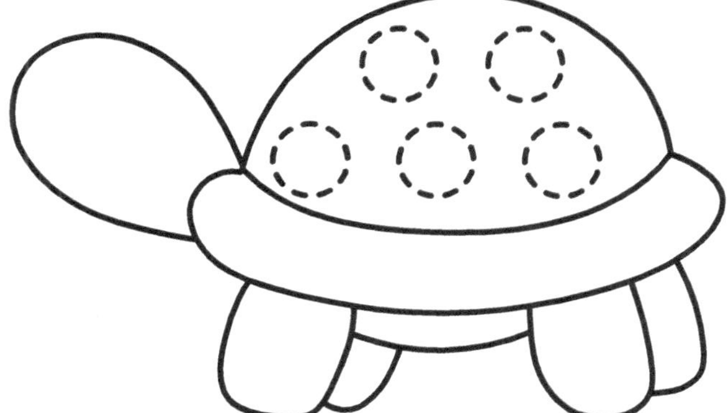

6

Make small circles to
decorate the shell

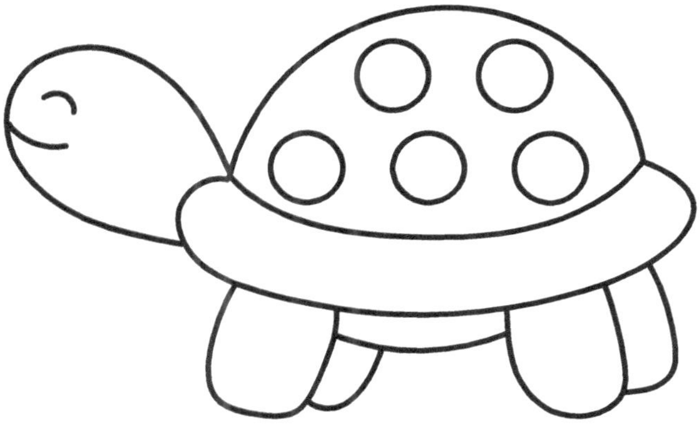

Make the eyes and
mouth to complete!

DUCK

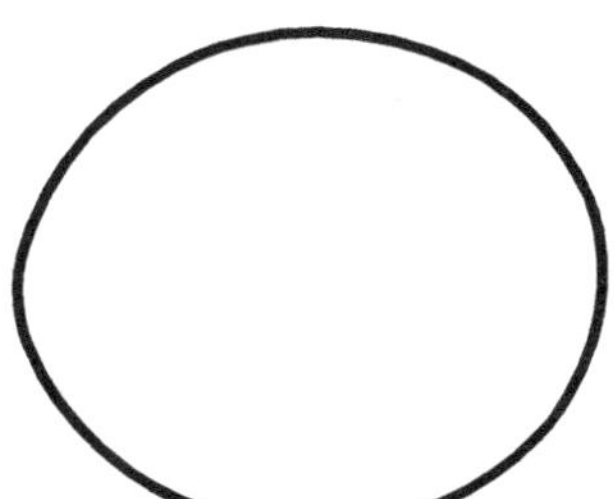

Draw a circular head

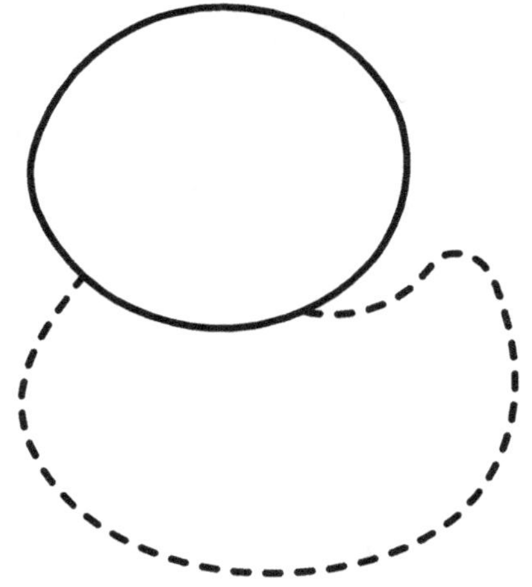

Now draw the body of the duck

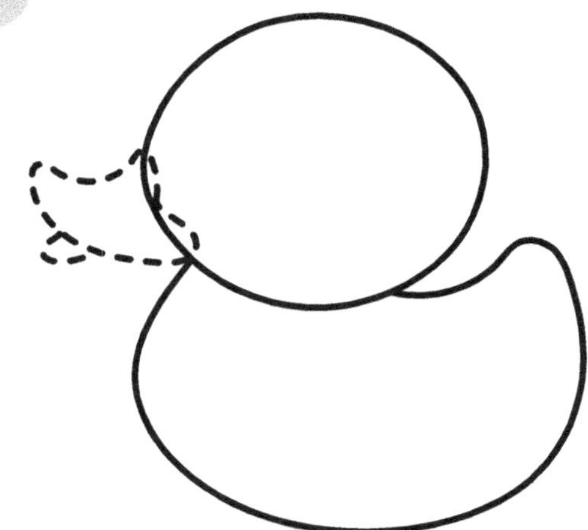

Draw the beak

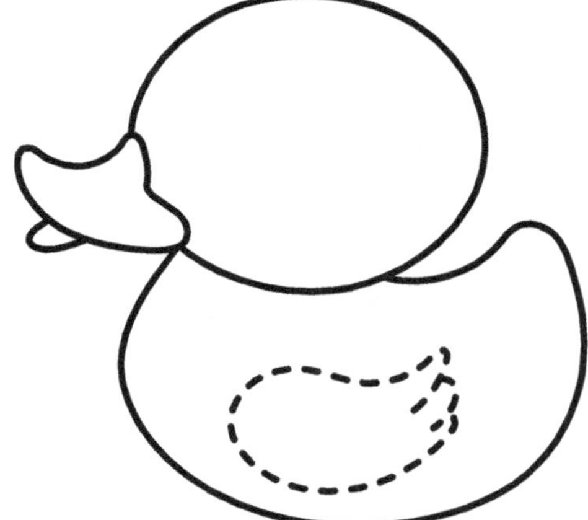

Make the feathers of the duck

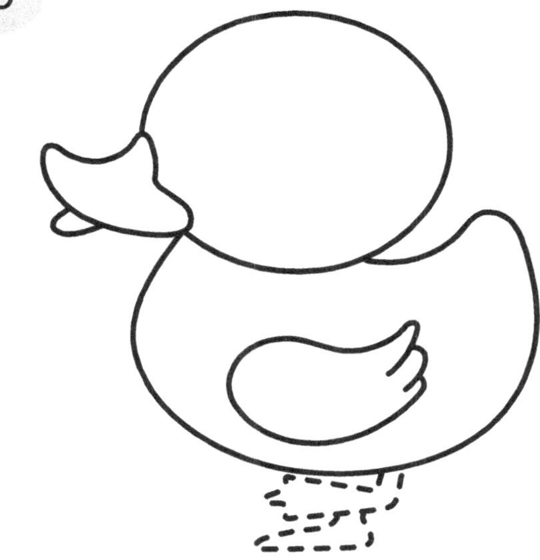

Make cute, webbed feet

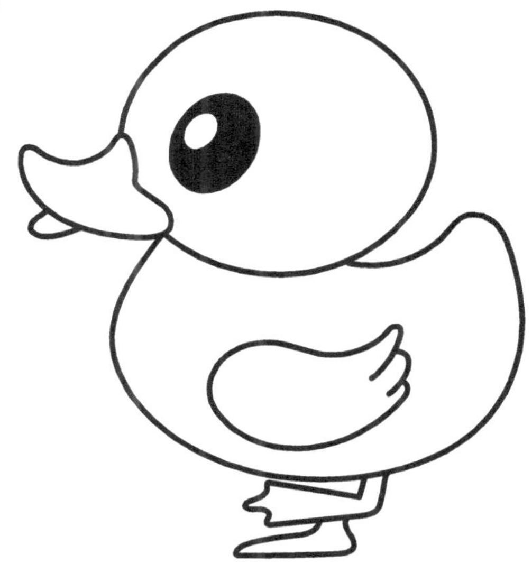

Draw the eye to
complete your duck!

KANGAROO

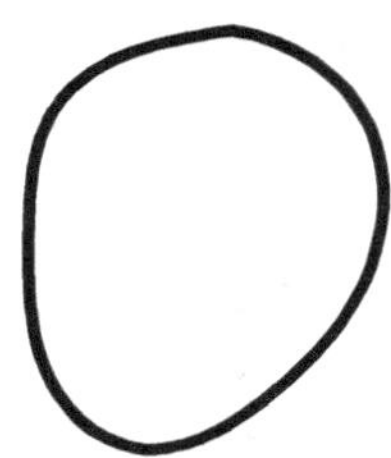

Draw an oval for the face

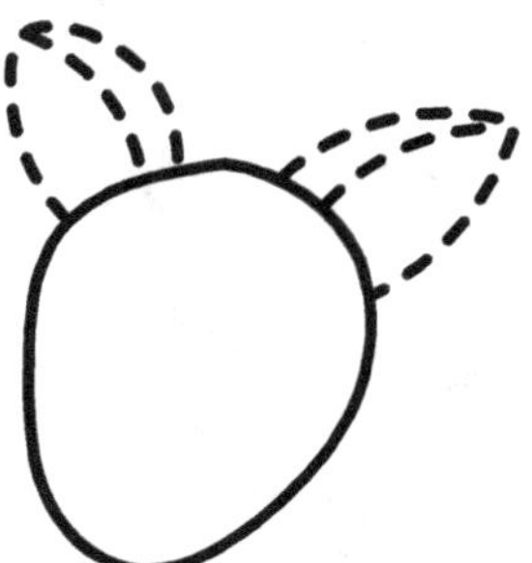

Draw two pointy ears

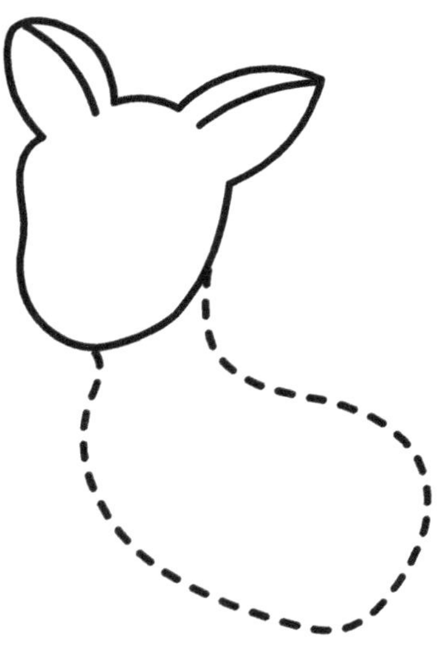

Draw a bigger
oval for the body

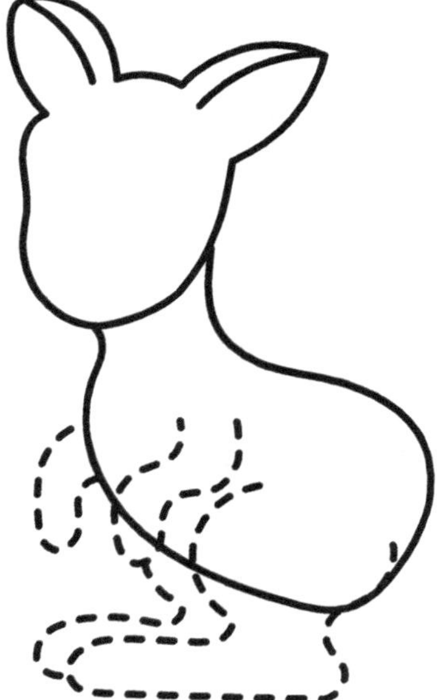

Draw four big limbs

5

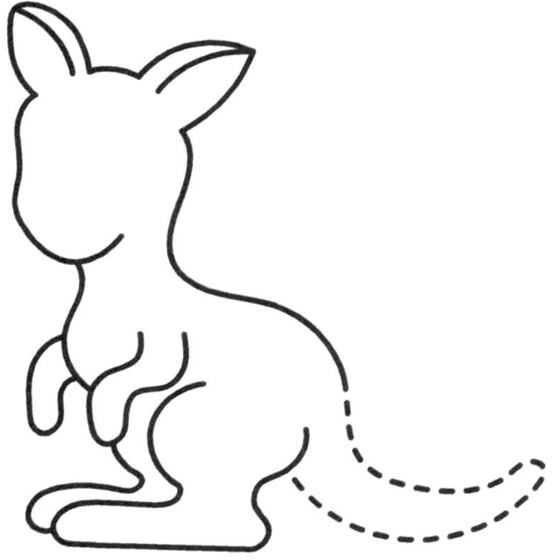

Draw a long tail

6

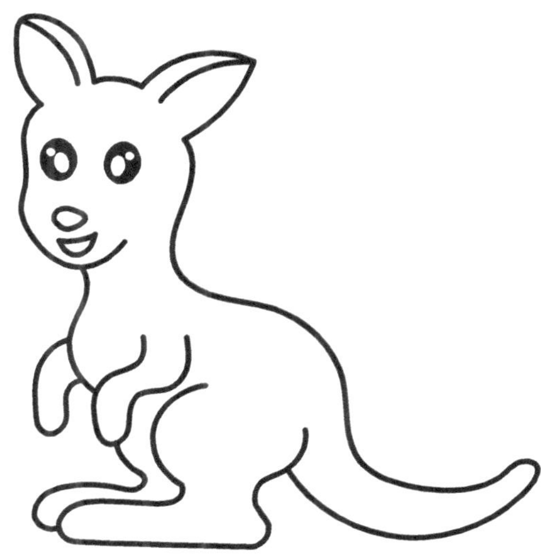

Draw an adorable
face to complete!

RABBIT

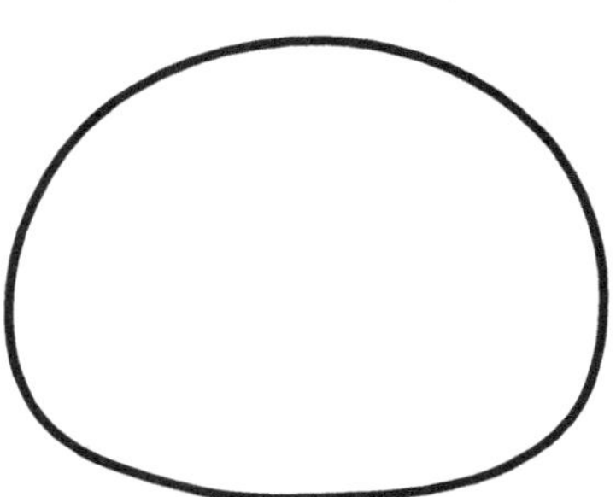

1 Start with a circular head

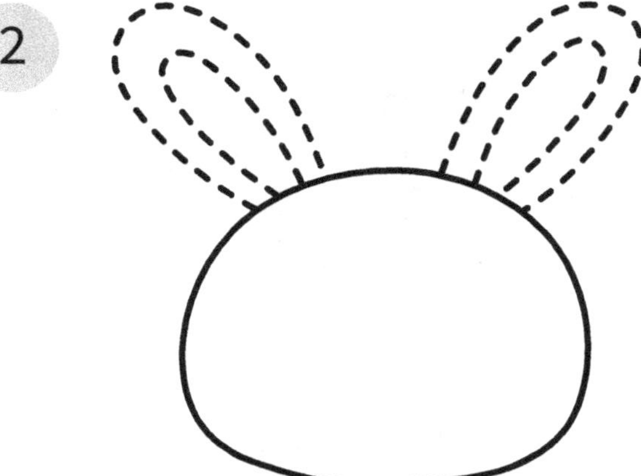

2 Draw two long ears

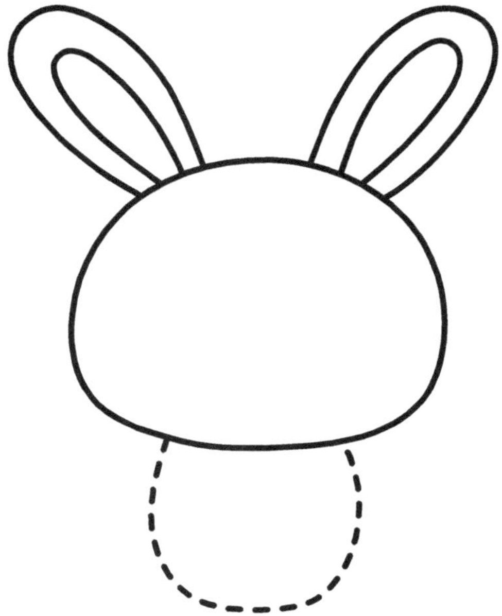

3 Draw an oval for the body

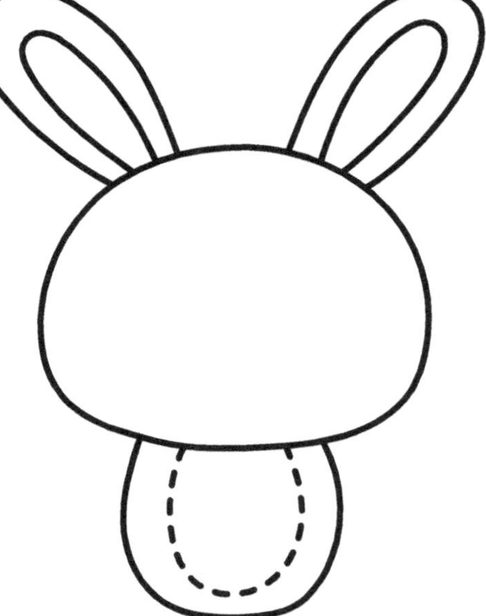

4 Make the outline of the fur

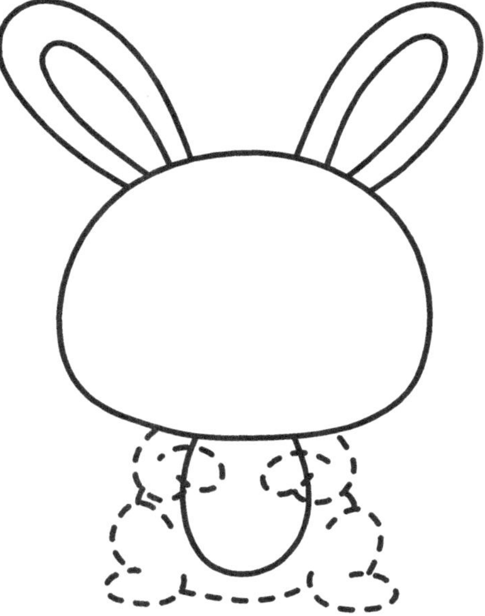

Draw four cute limbs

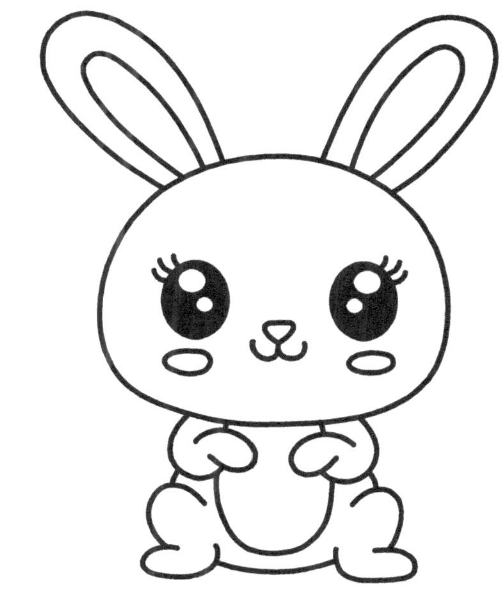

Make the face
to complete the rabbit!

PANDA

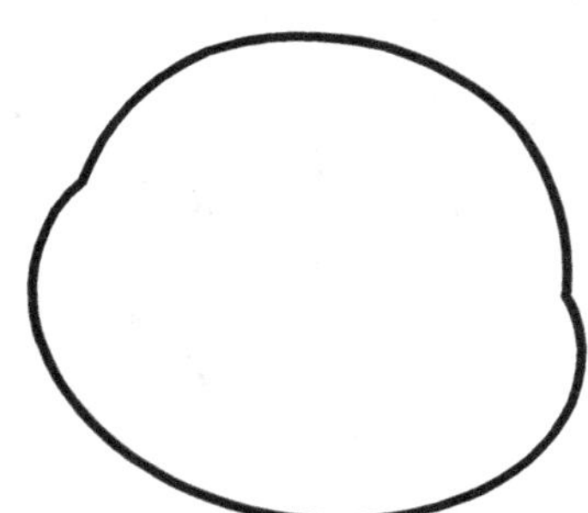

Draw a circular head

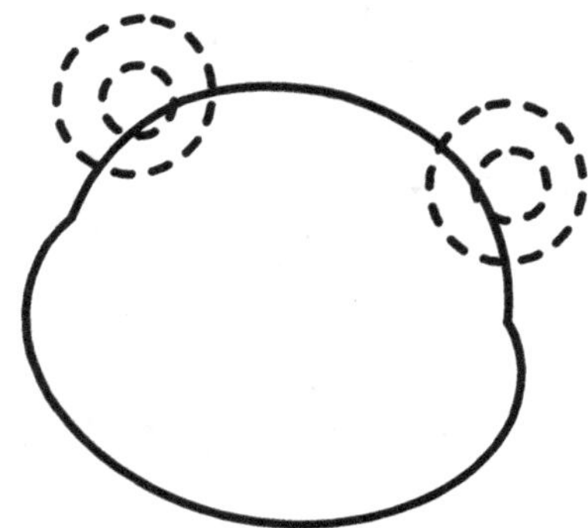

Make two concentric
circles for each ear

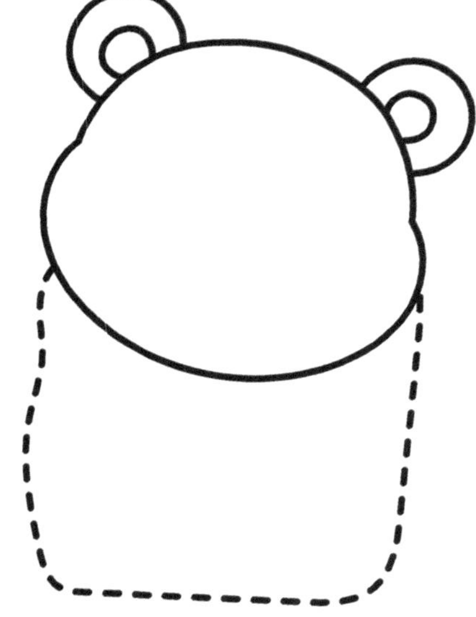

Make a rectangular body

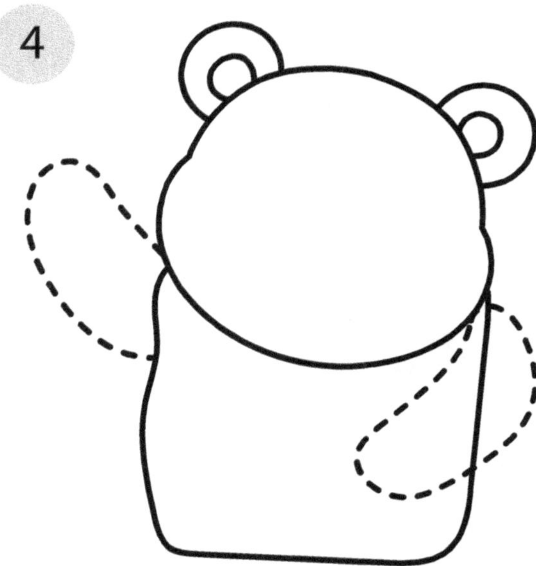

Draw two chubby hands

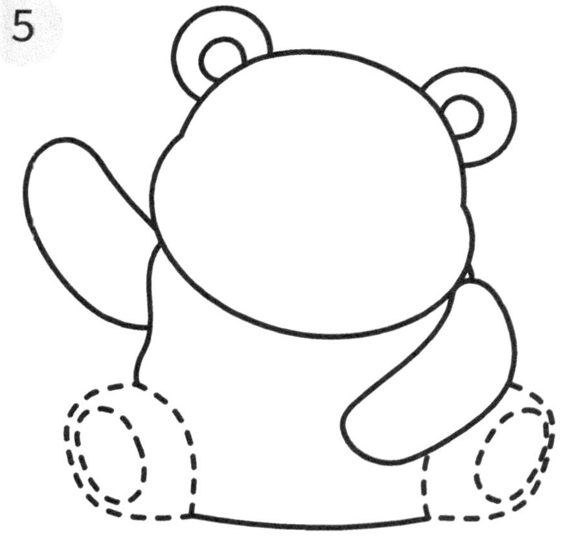

Make two cute feet

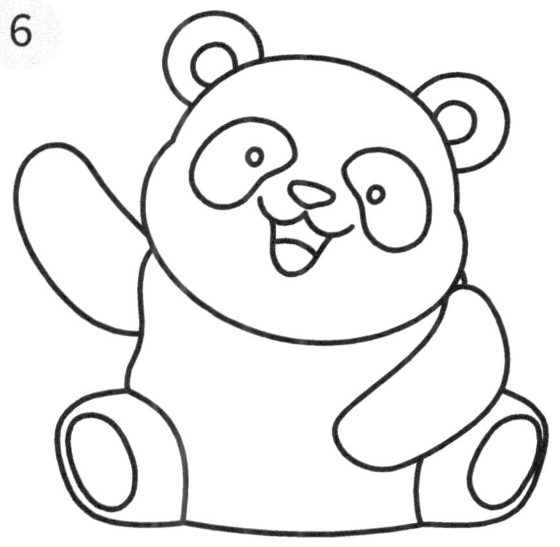

Draw the face
to get your panda!

FROG

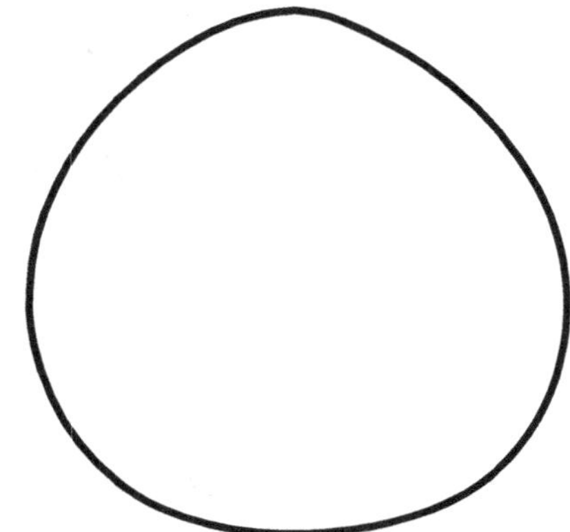

Start with a circular body

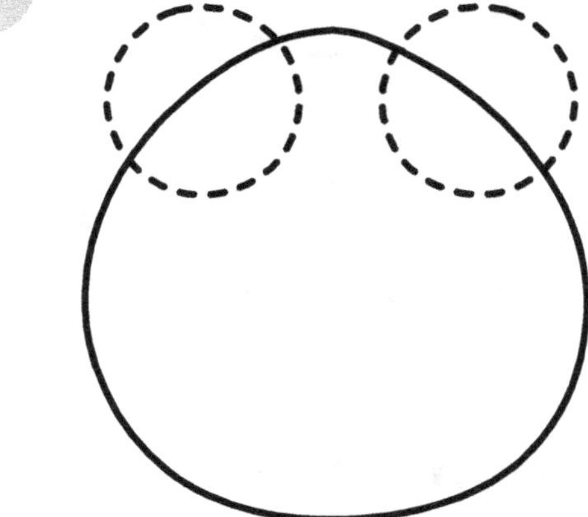

Make two circles
for **eye sockets**

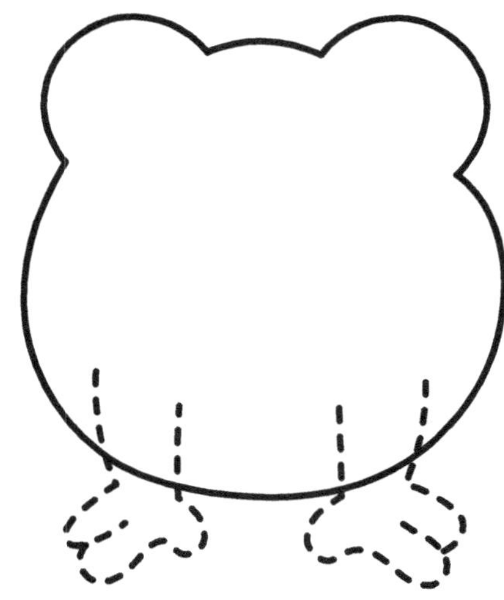

Draw two front legs

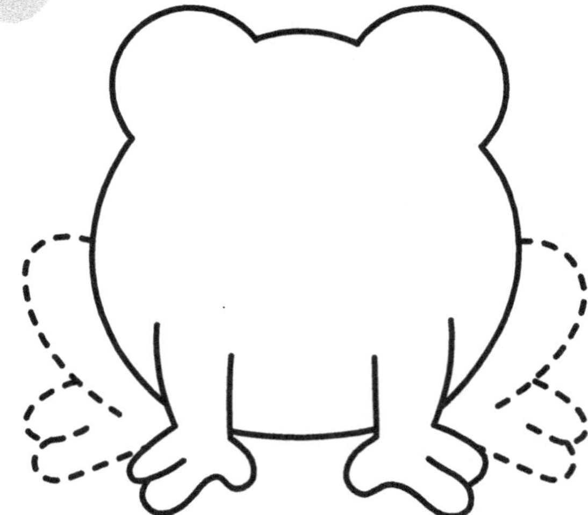

Now make two hind legs

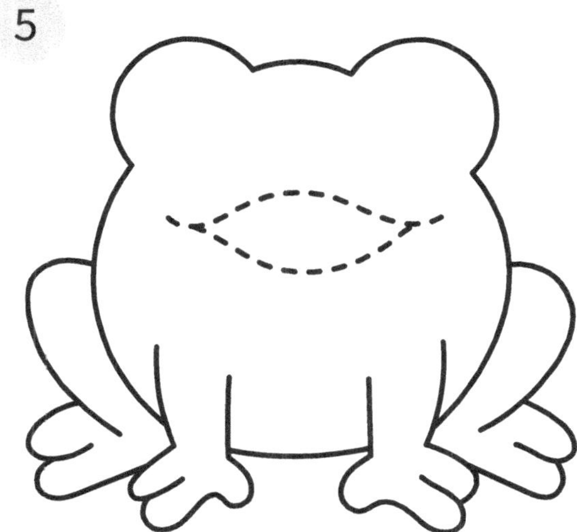

5

Draw a big smile

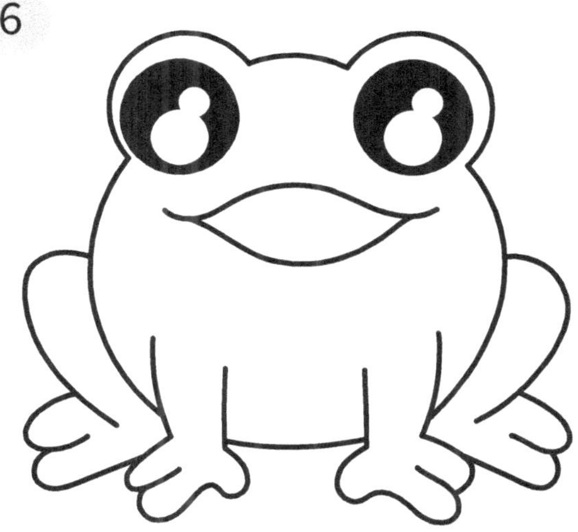

6

Make adorable
eyes to finish!

TIGER

1

Star with a circular,
furry face

2

Draw rectangular ears

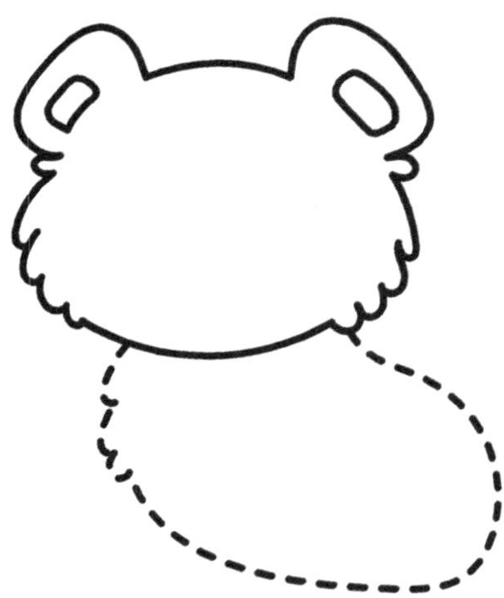

3

Draw an oval
for the body

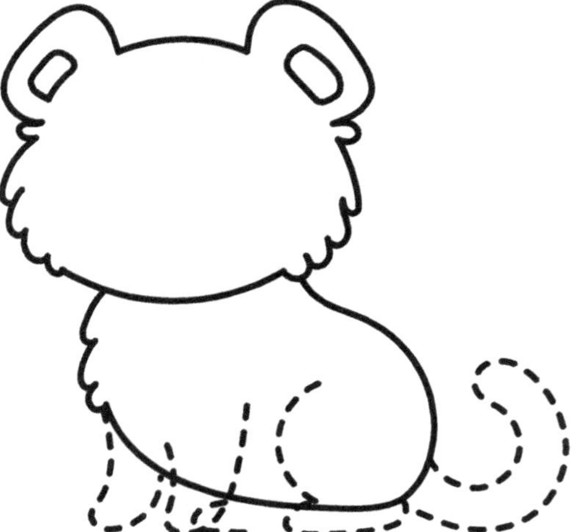

4

Draw four legs
and a long tail

5

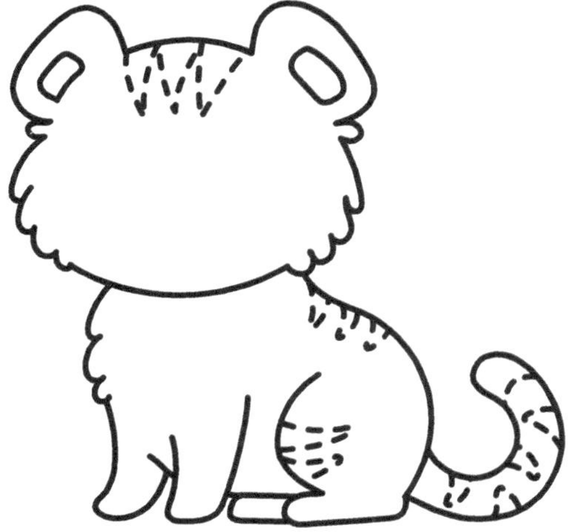

Make the stripes

6

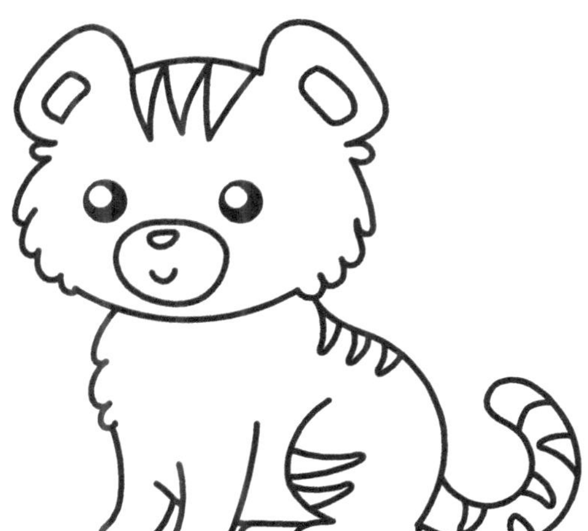

Make a cute face
to complete your tiger!

BEE

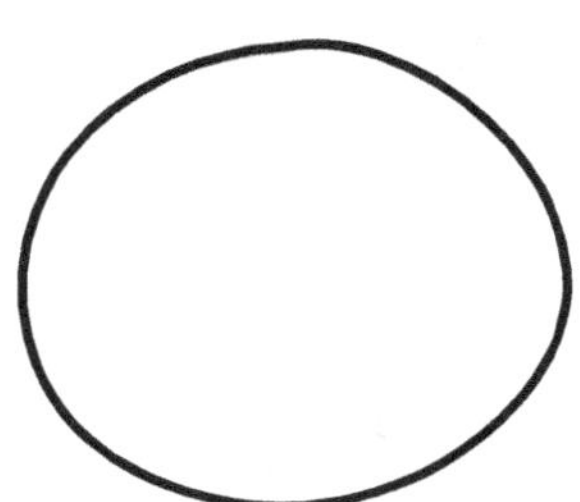

Start by drawing
a circular head

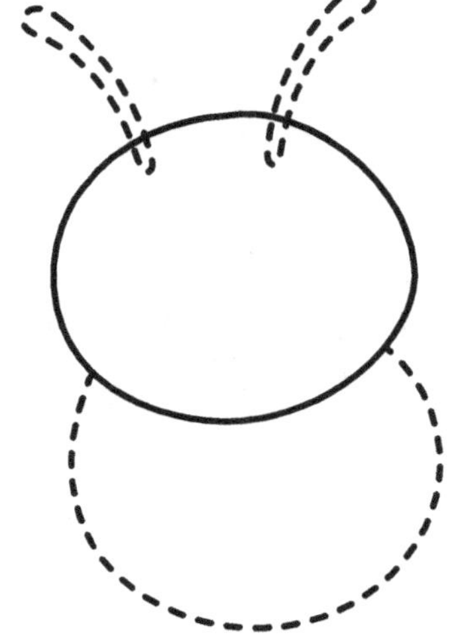

Draw two long antennas
and oval for the body

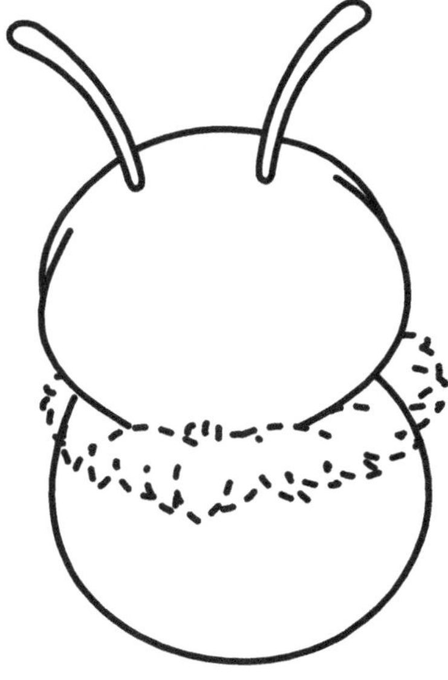

Draw the fur
around the neck

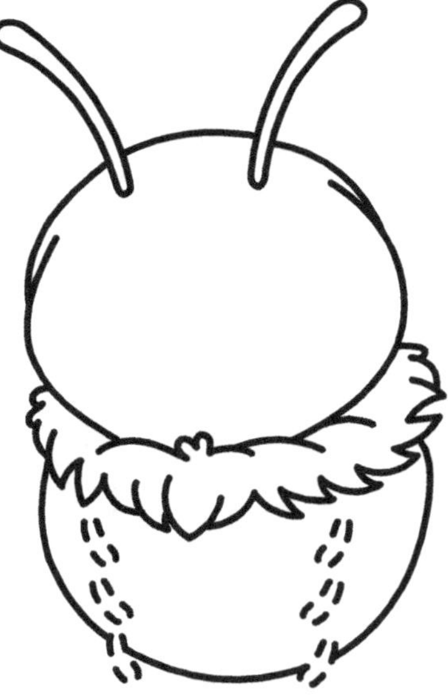

Make six tiny legs

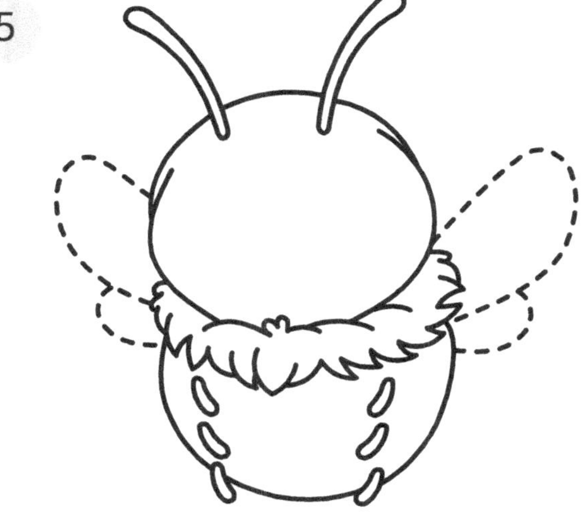

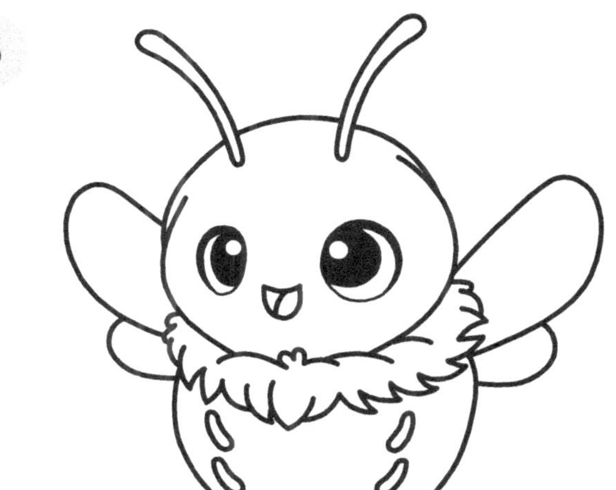

5

Draw the wings
of the bee

6

Make a cute
face to complete!

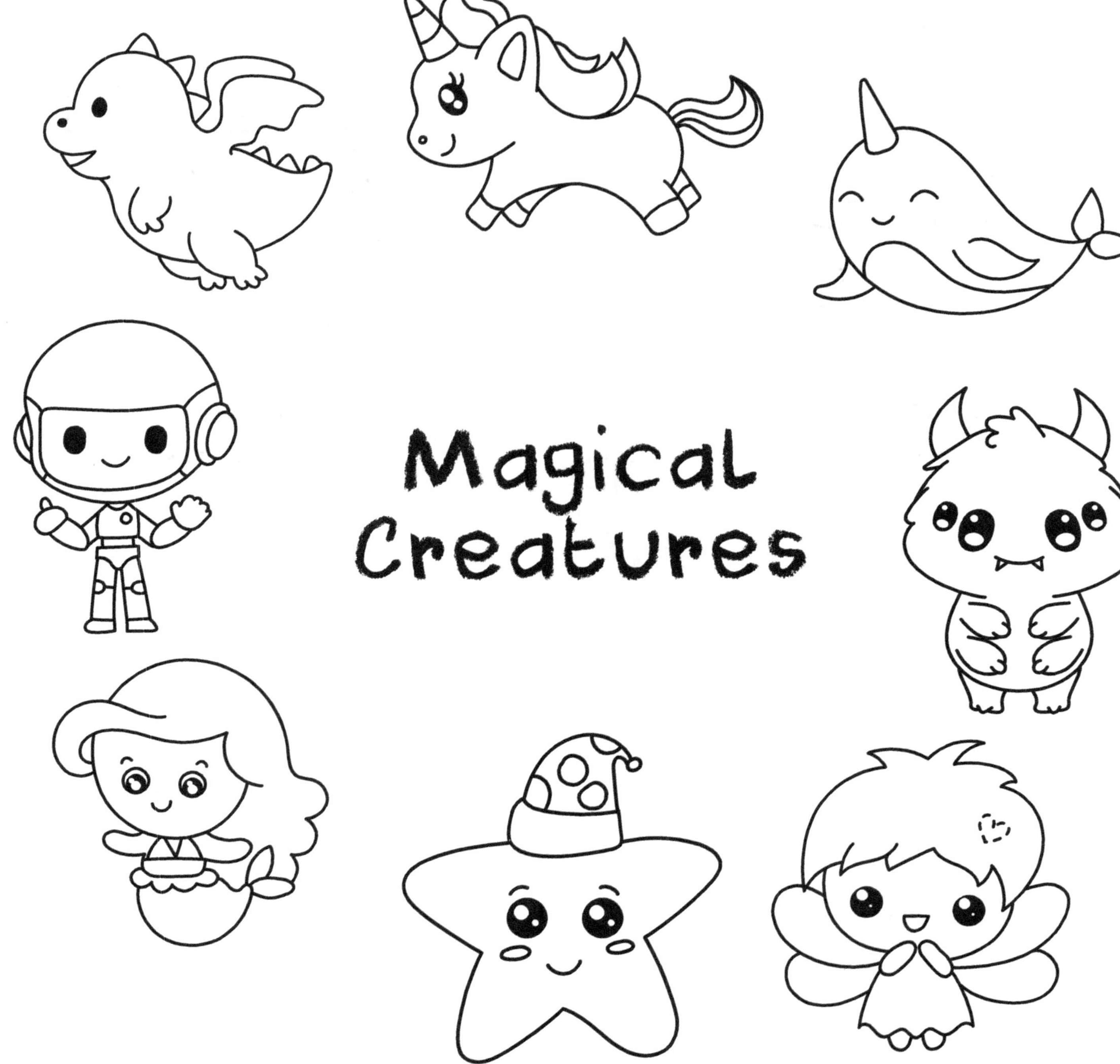

Magical
Creatures

DRAGON

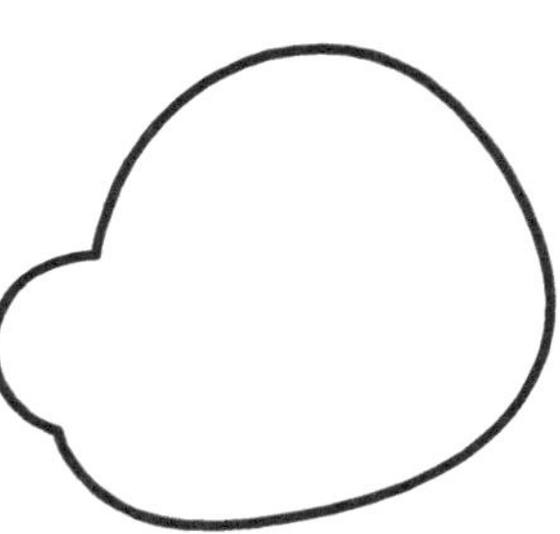

Start by drawing the head

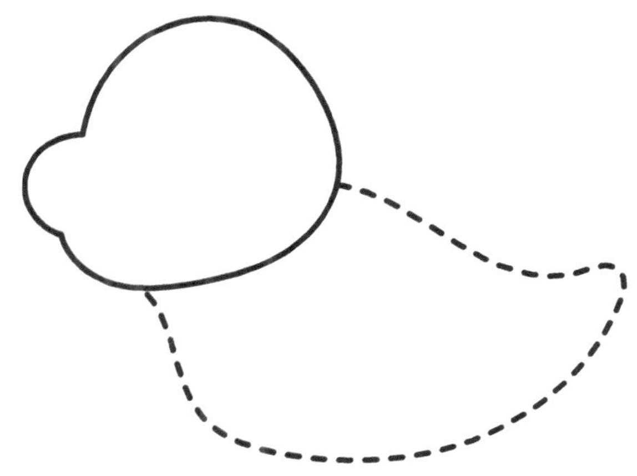

Draw the body

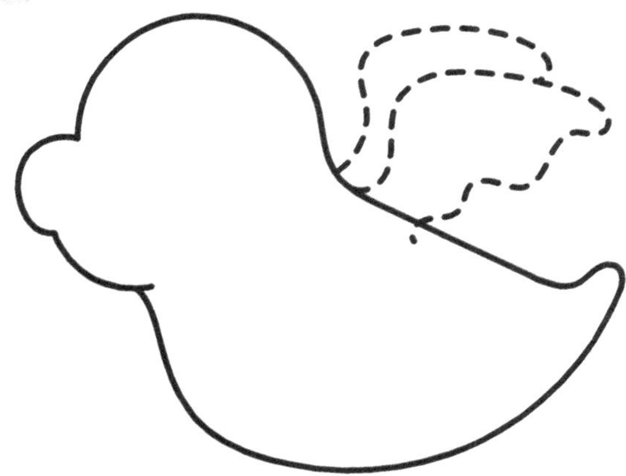

Make two small wings

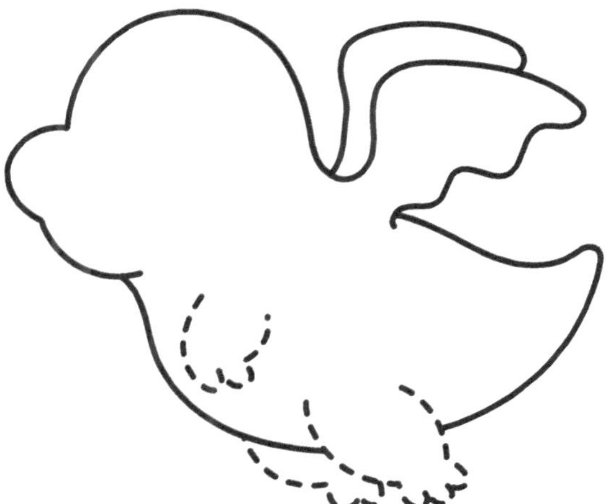

Draw four cute limbs

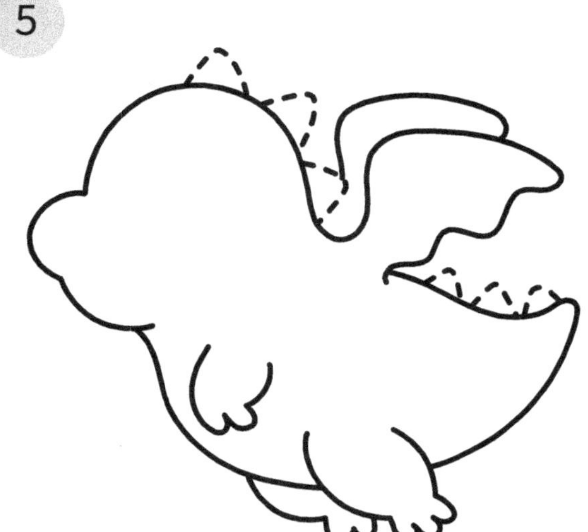

Draw tiny triangular scales

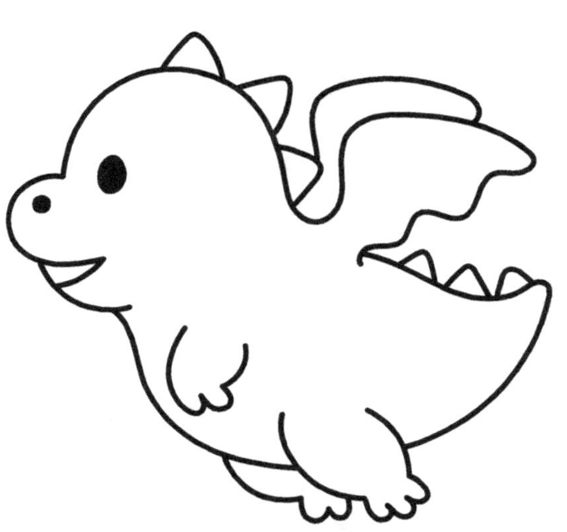

Draw the face to complete!

UNICORN

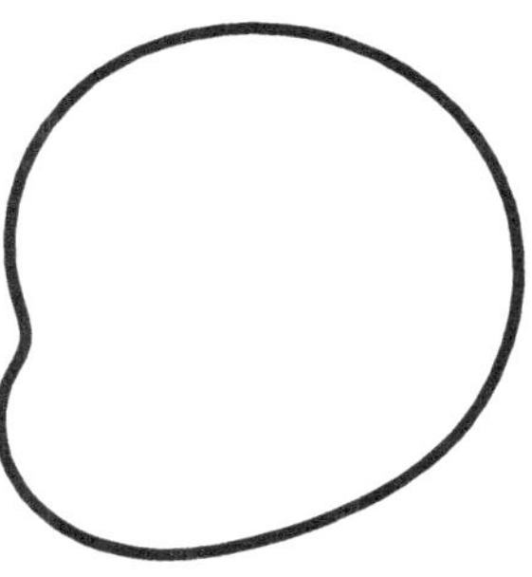

Start by drawing
the head of the unicorn

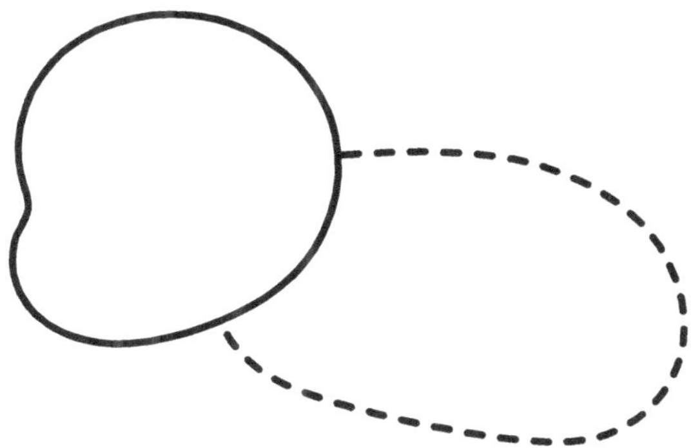

Draw an oval for the body

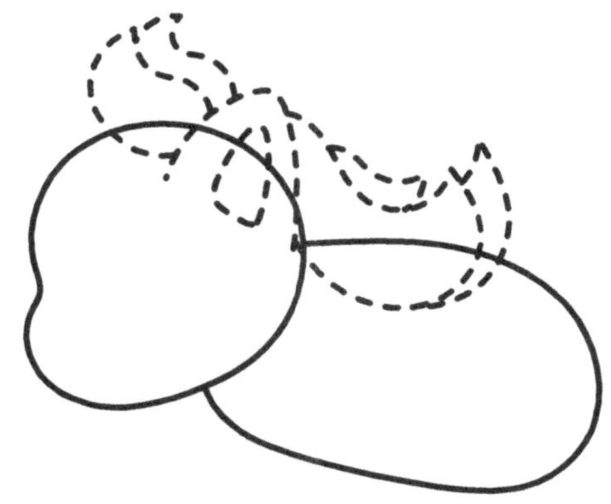

Draw the ear and hair

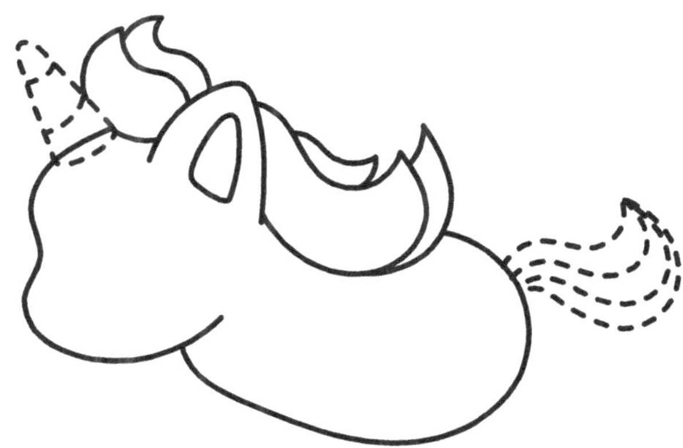

Draw the tail and the horn

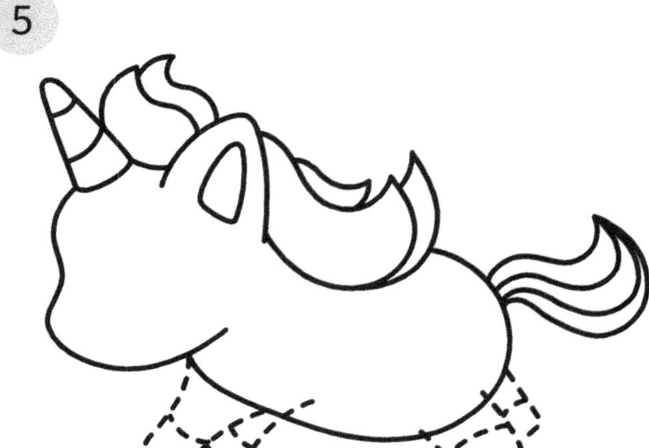

Make four cute legs

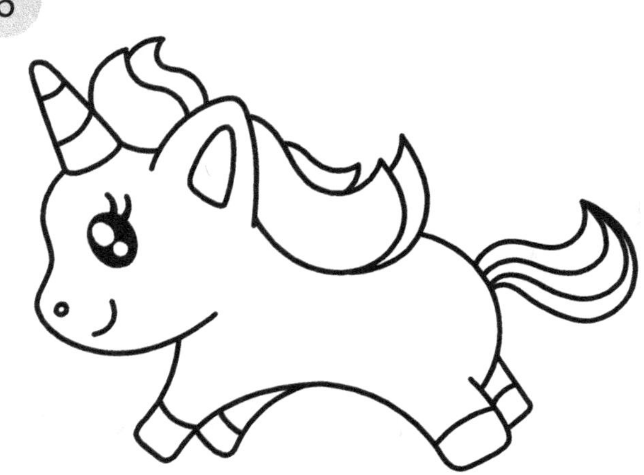

Draw the face to
complete your unicorn!

NARWHAL

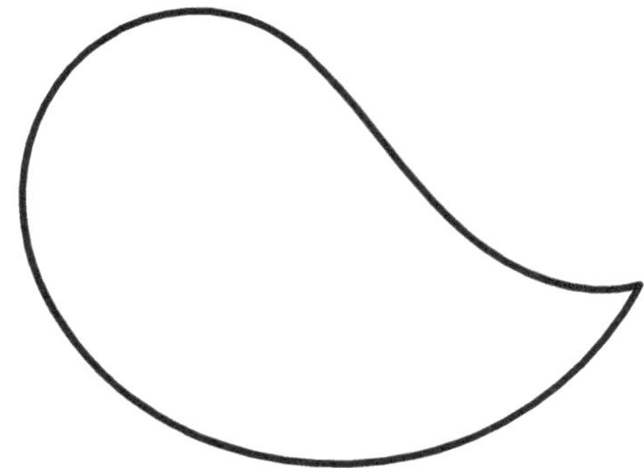

Begin by drawing a
balloon-shaped body

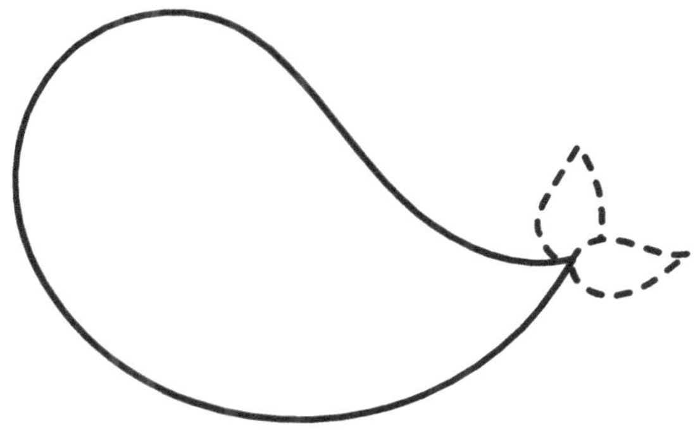

Draw a cute tail

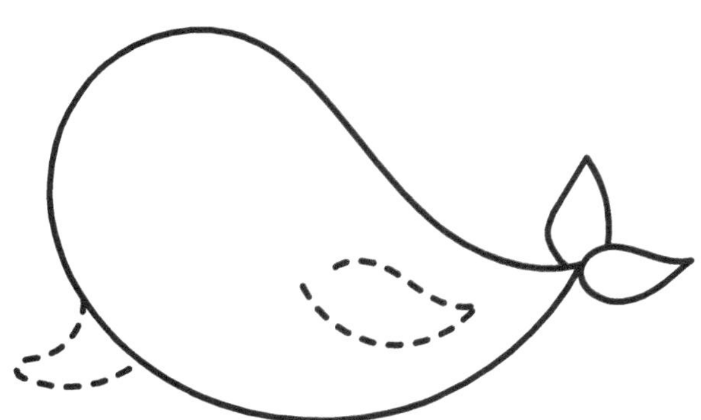

Draw two small fins

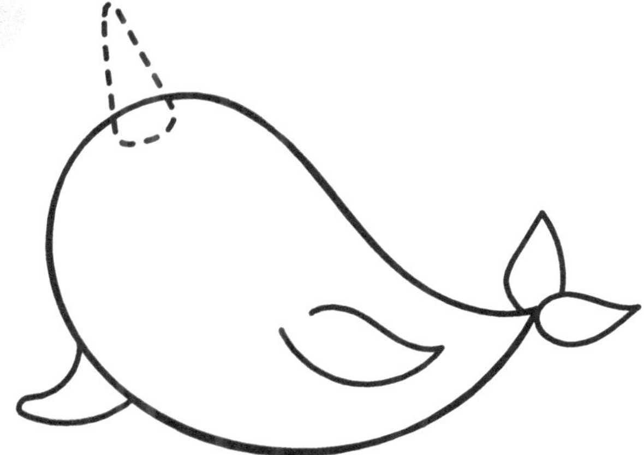

Make a tiny horn on
narwhal's head

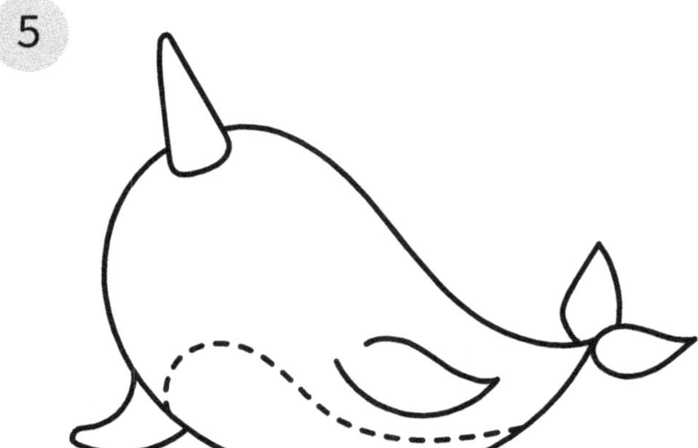

Now add details

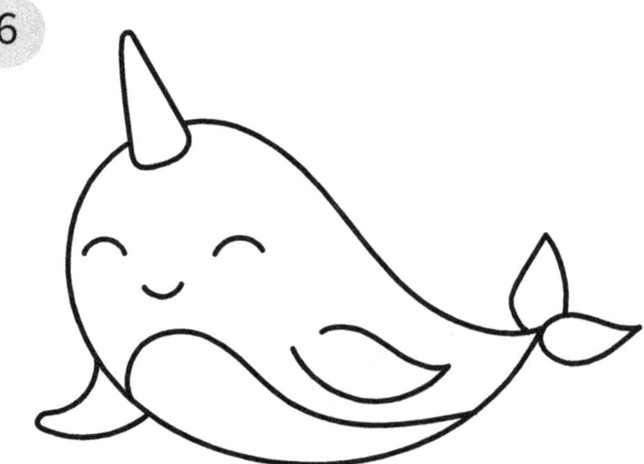

Make a sweet
face to complete!

FAIRY

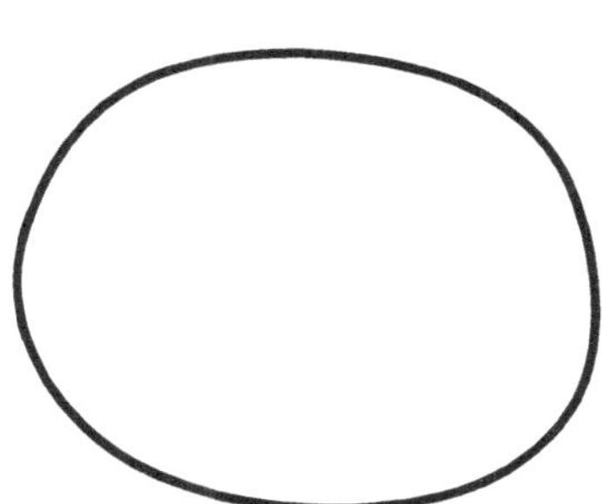

Draw a cute circular face

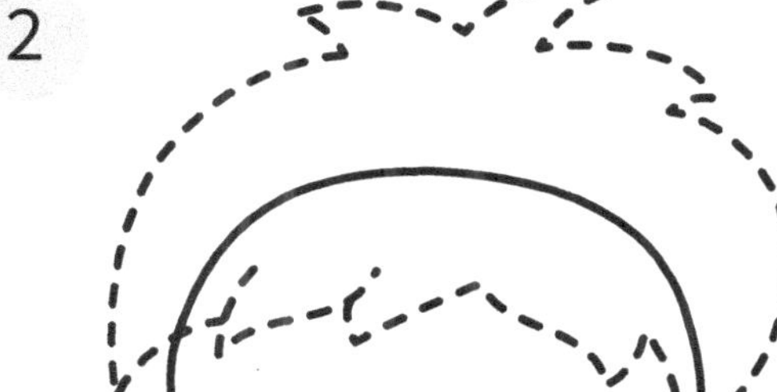

Make the hair of the fairy

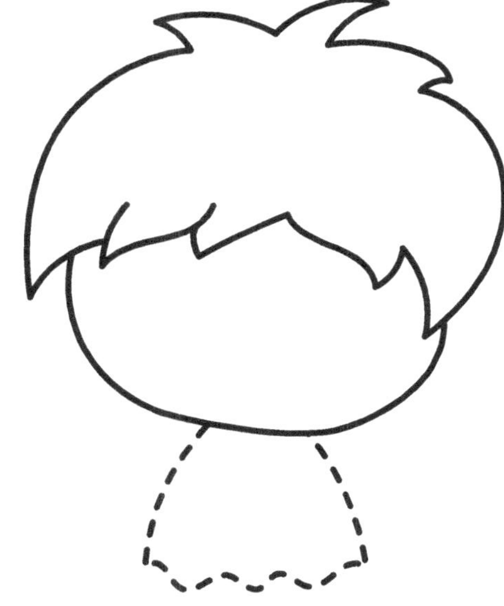

Draw a triangular wavy dress

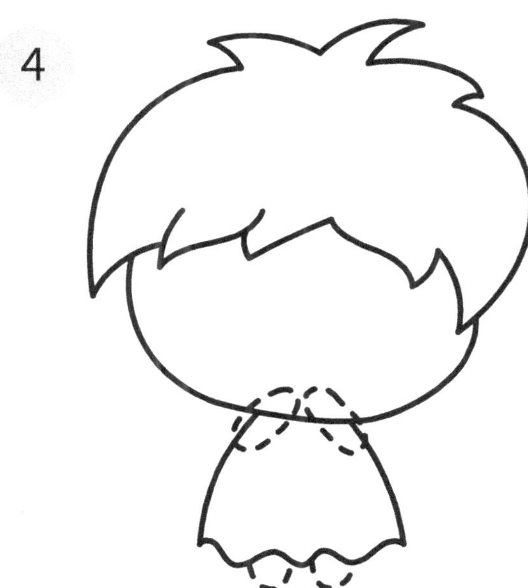

Draw two cute arms and feet

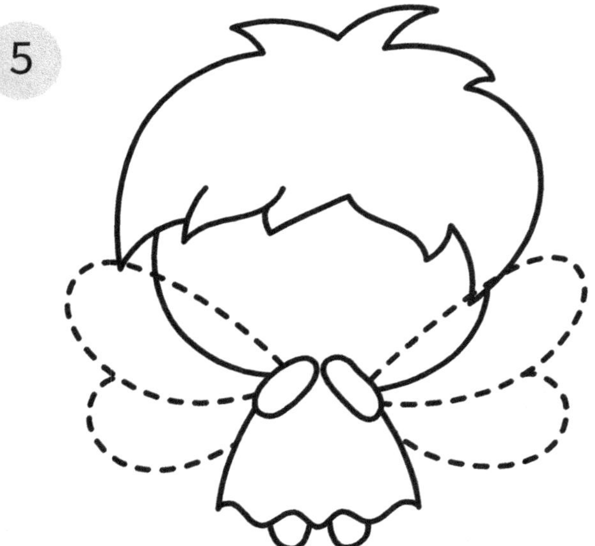

Draw the wings of the fairy

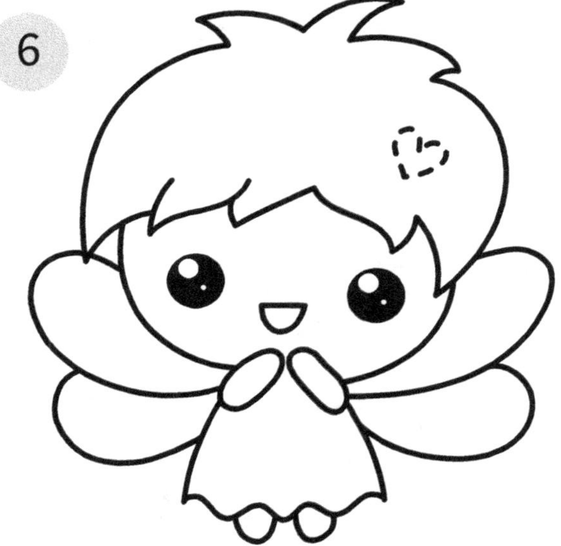

Draw a heart clip in her hair
and the face to complete!

MERMAID

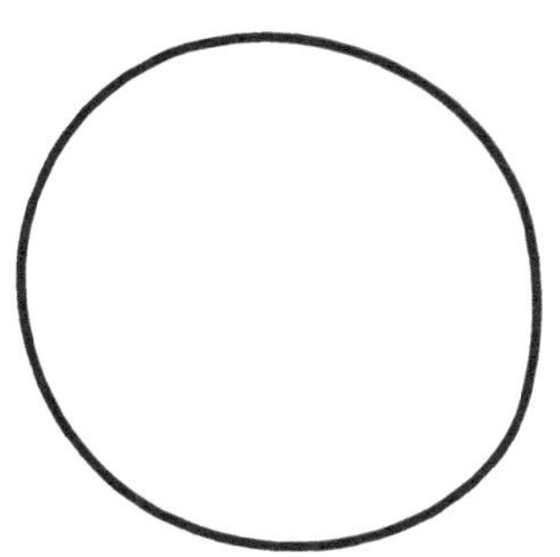

Make a circular face

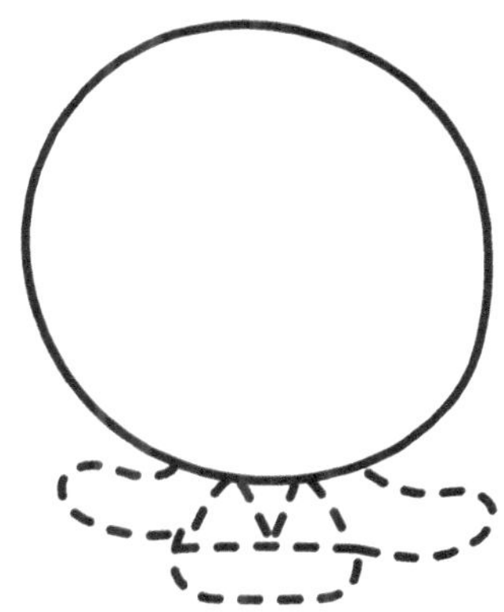

Draw the upper body

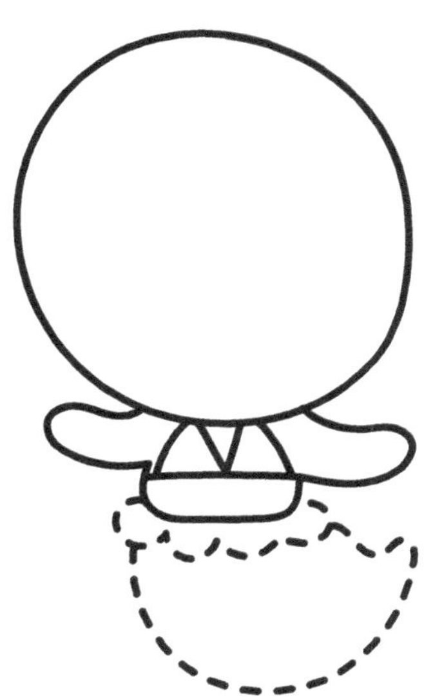

Draw the frill and tail

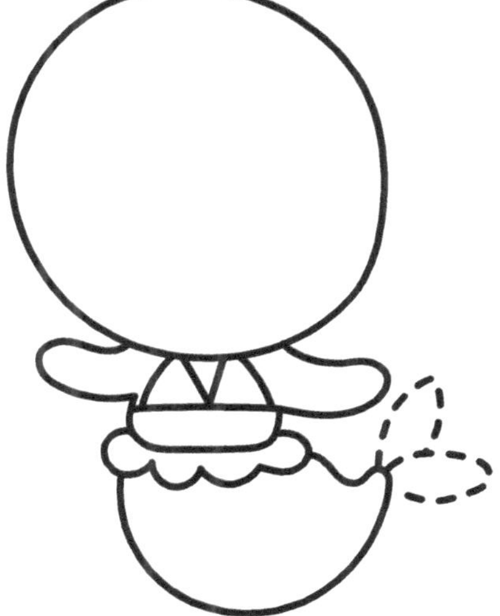

Draw two small fins at
the end of the tail

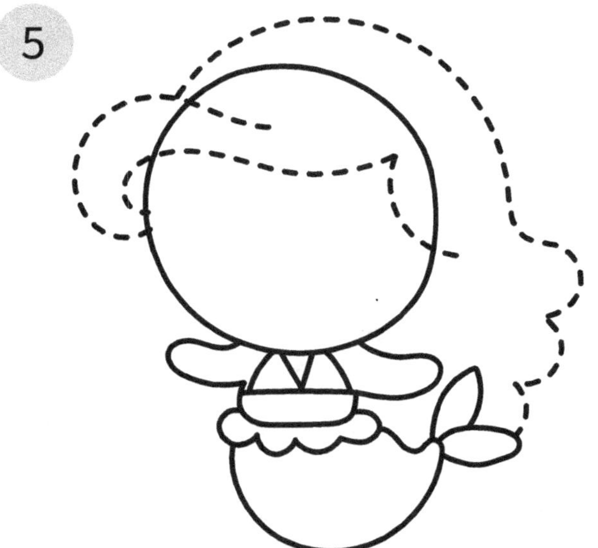
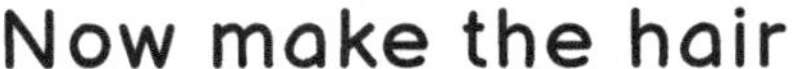

Now make the hair

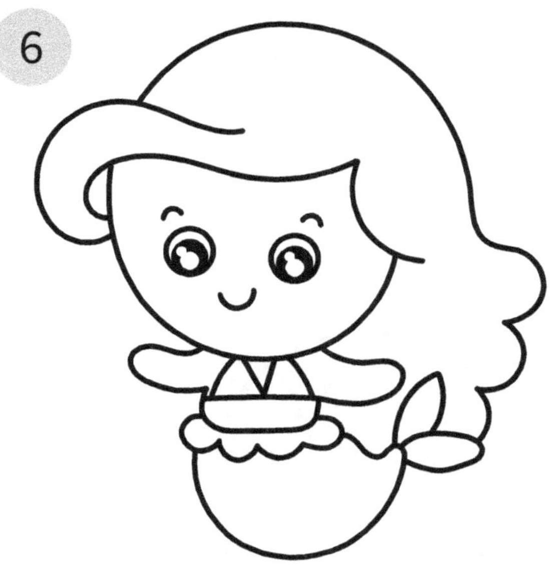

Draw the face to complete!

ROBOT

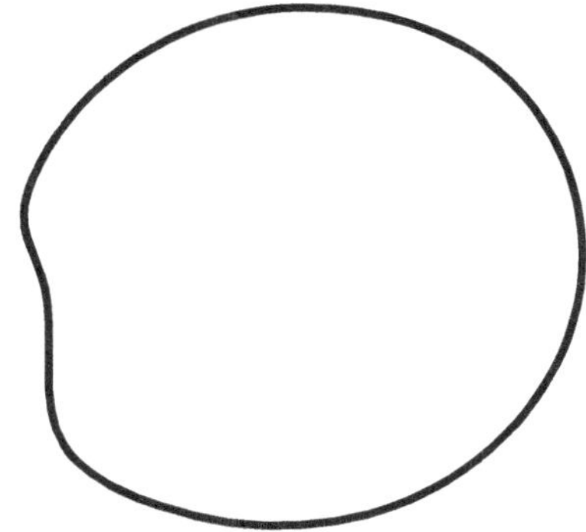

1

Start with a circular helmet

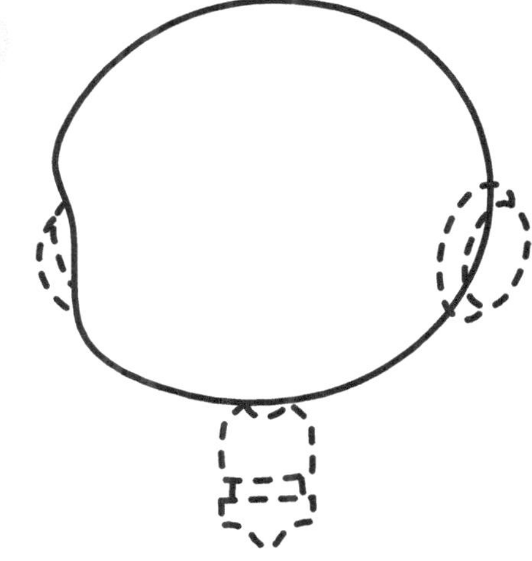

2

Draw the ear and it's suit

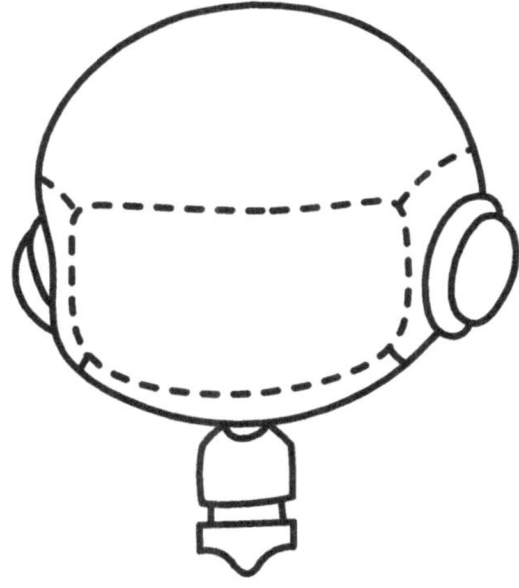

3

Make the glass
of the helmet

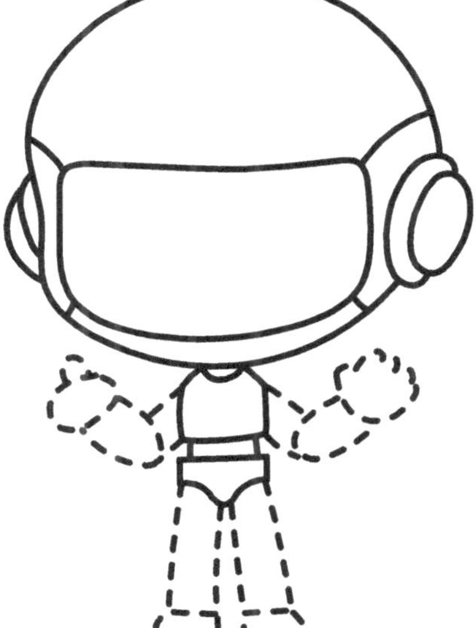

4

Draw two arms and legs

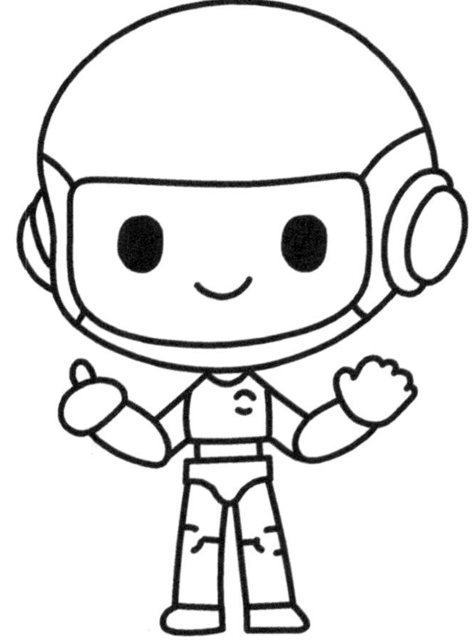

5

Add details to
the robot suit

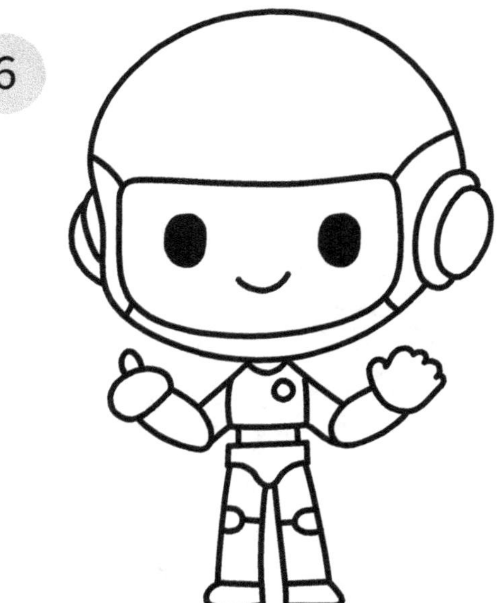

6

Draw a cute
face to complete!

MONSTER

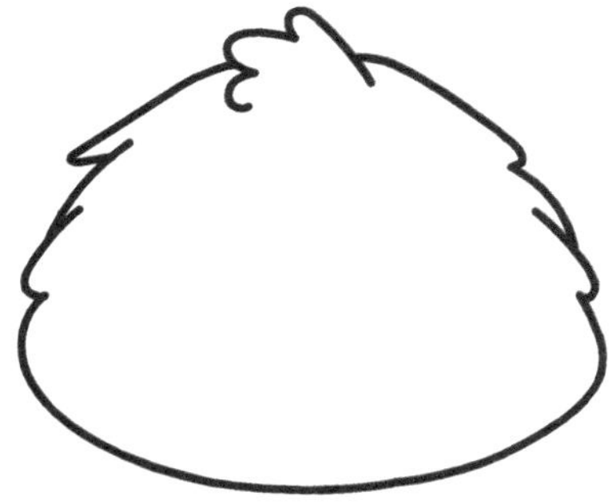

First draw a circular head with a little fur

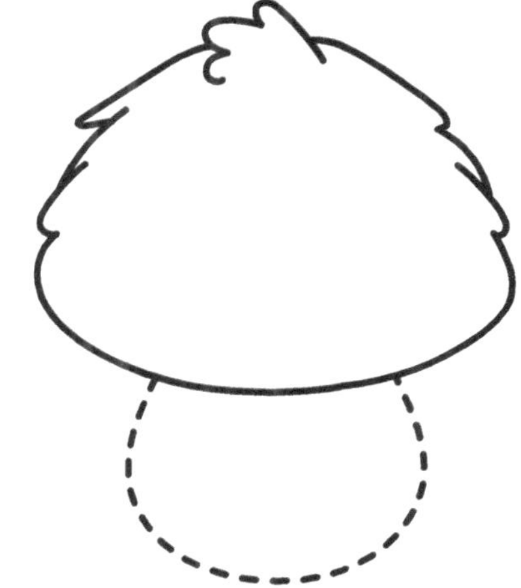

Draw an oval for the body

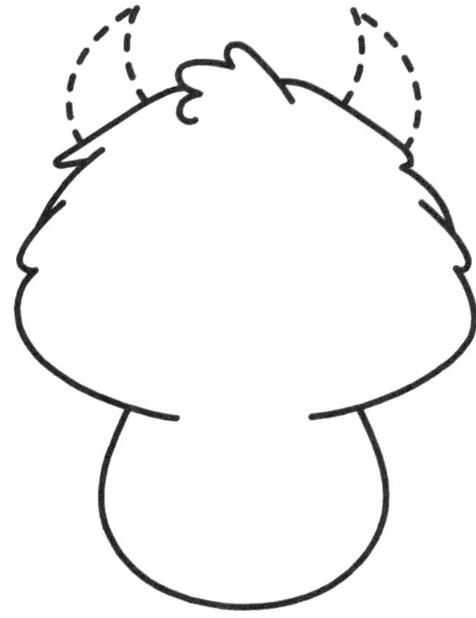

Draw two cute horns

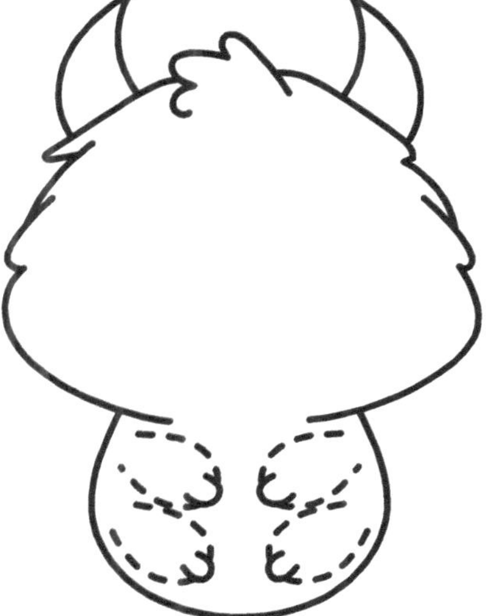

Make four small hands

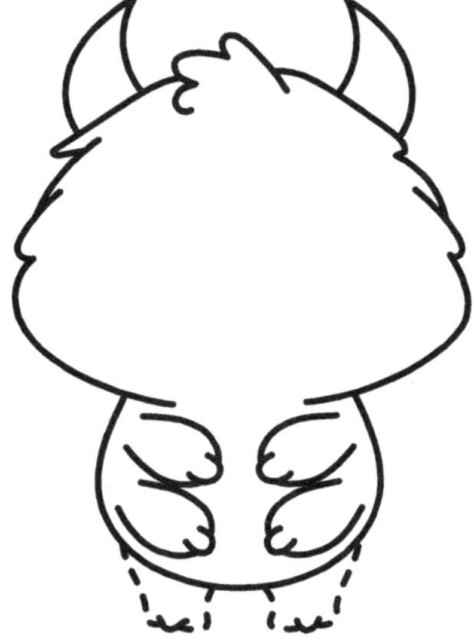

5

Make two tiny legs

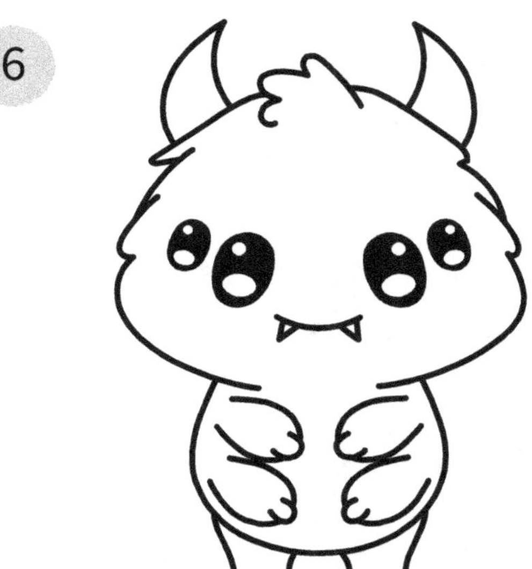

6

Make four eyes and two small teeth with a smile to complete!

STAR

1

Make five triangles

2

Make the base of its hat

3

Draw the rest of the hat

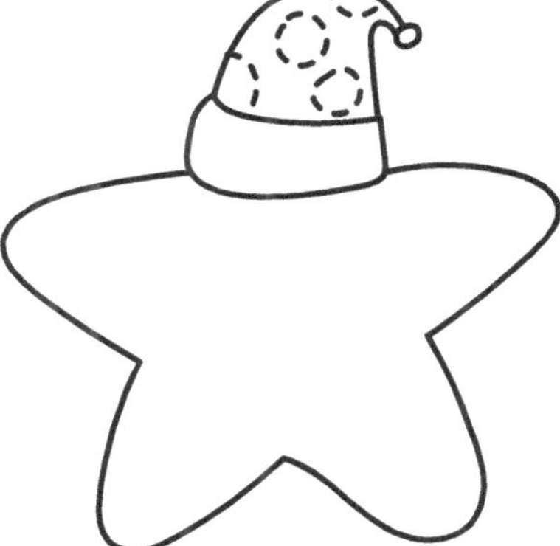

4

Make circles on the hat

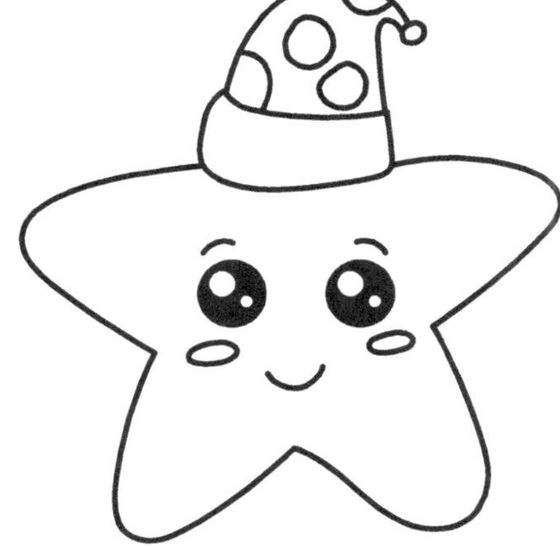

5

Draw a cute face
to complete your star!

DINOSAUR

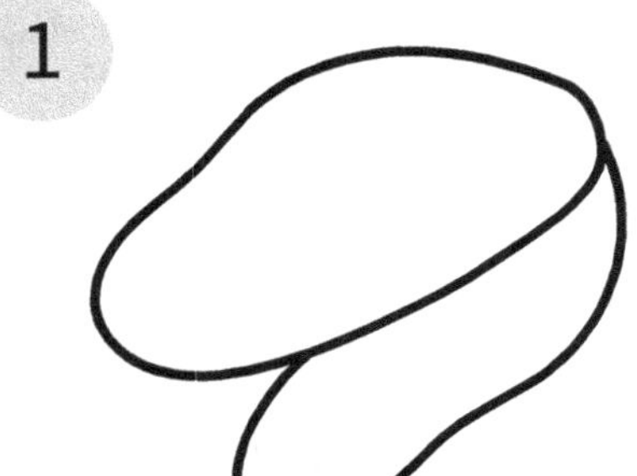

1

Draw two ovals
for the face

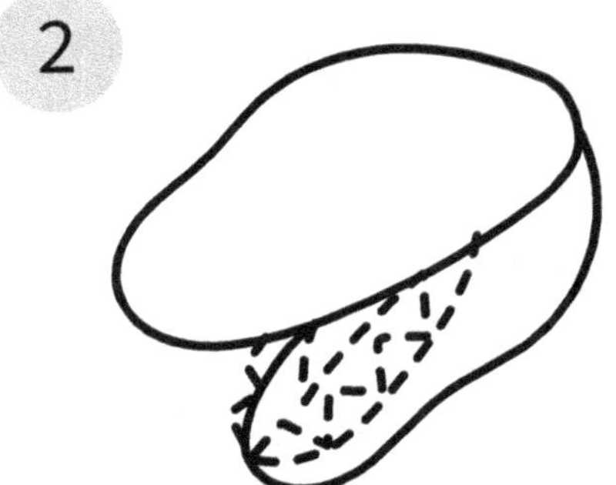

2

Now draw the
jaw and tongue

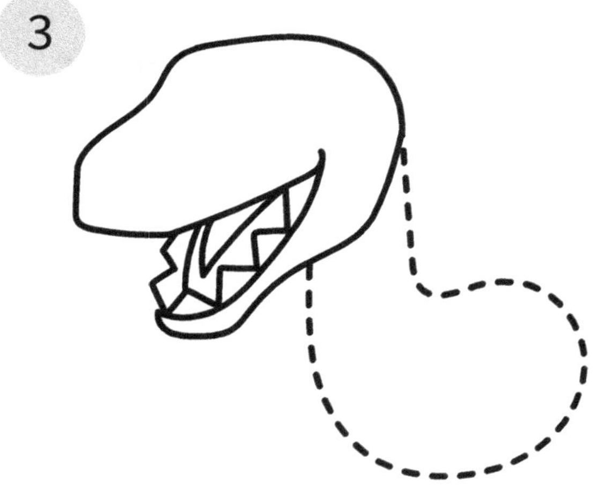

3

Draw a bigger
oval for the body

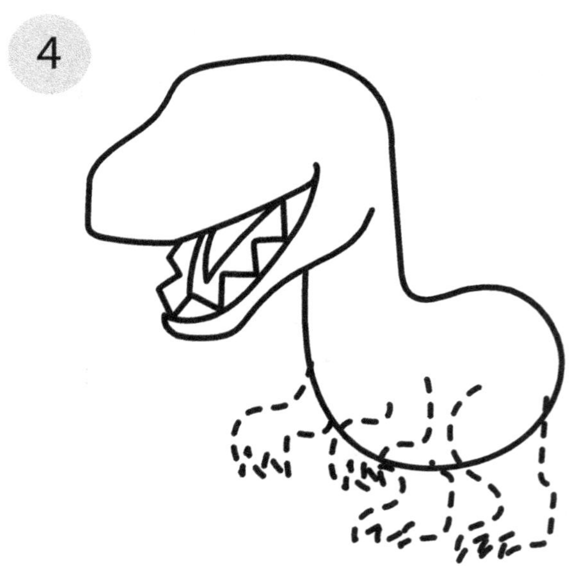

4

Draw four legs
with pointy nails

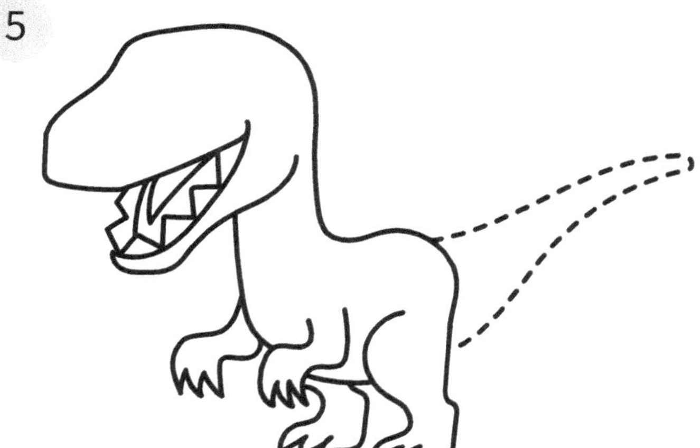

Draw a long tail

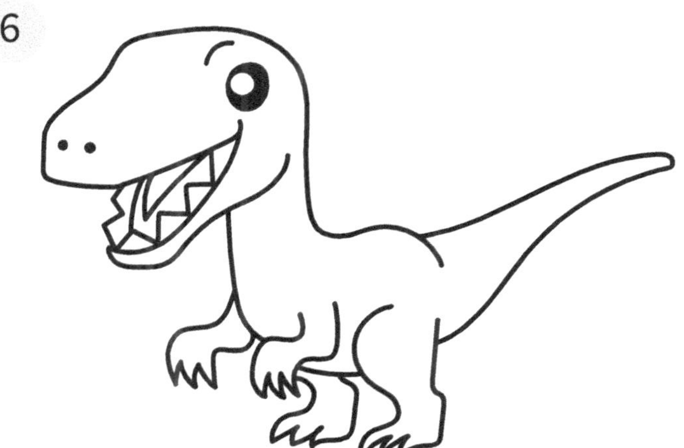

Draw the eyes and nose to complete!

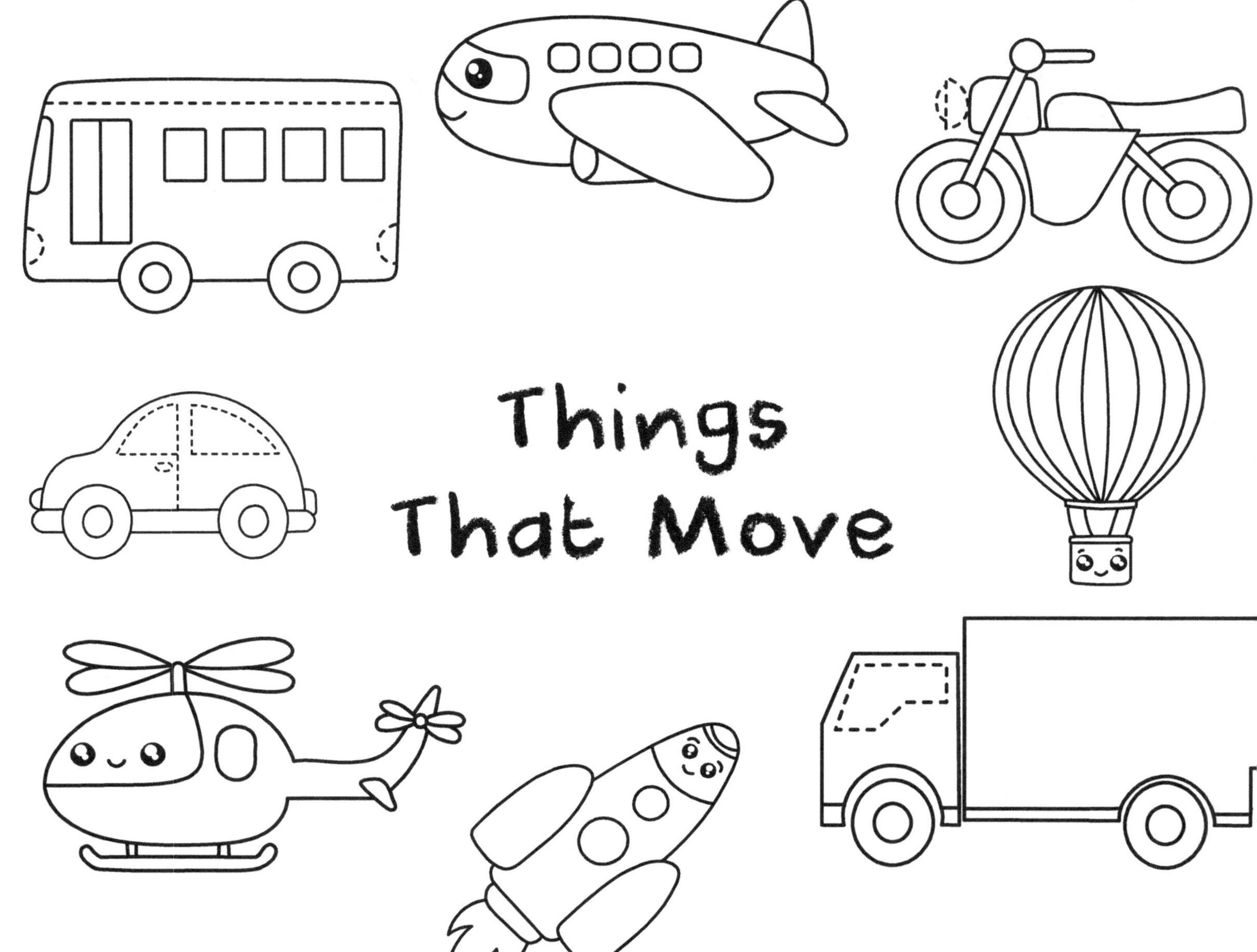
Things
That Move

BUS

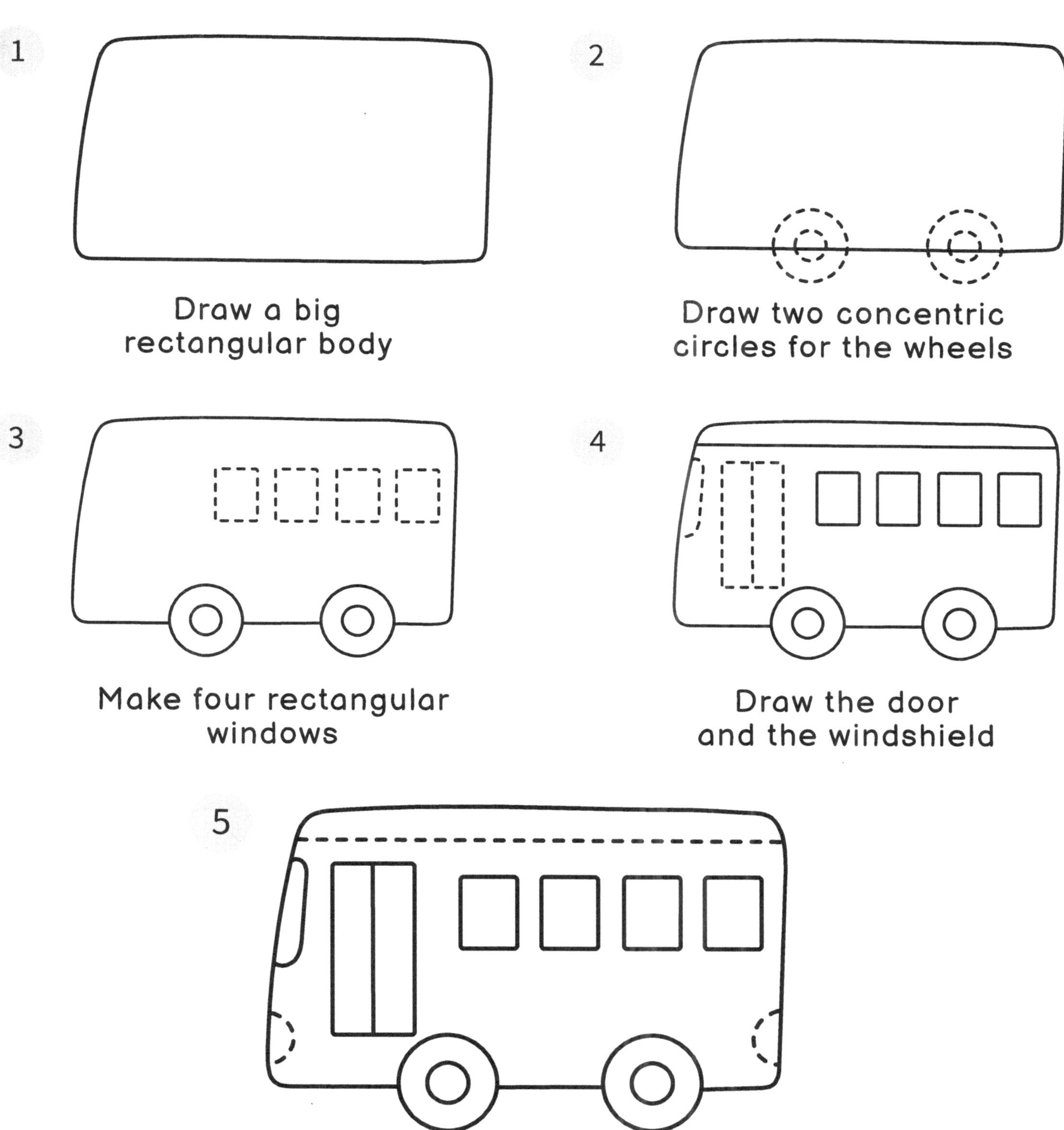

1. Draw a big rectangular body

2. Draw two concentric circles for the wheels

3. Make four rectangular windows

4. Draw the door and the windshield

5. Draw the lights and a line above the windows to complete!

CAR

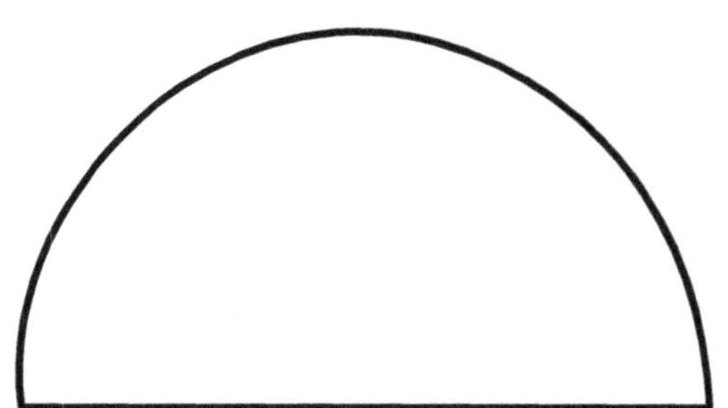

Draw a semi circle

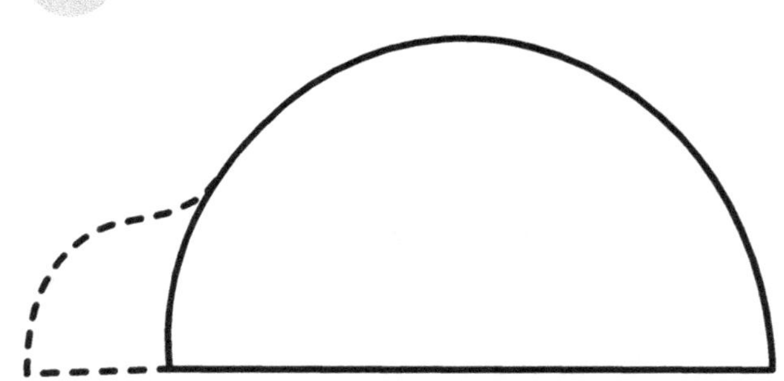

Draw the bumper

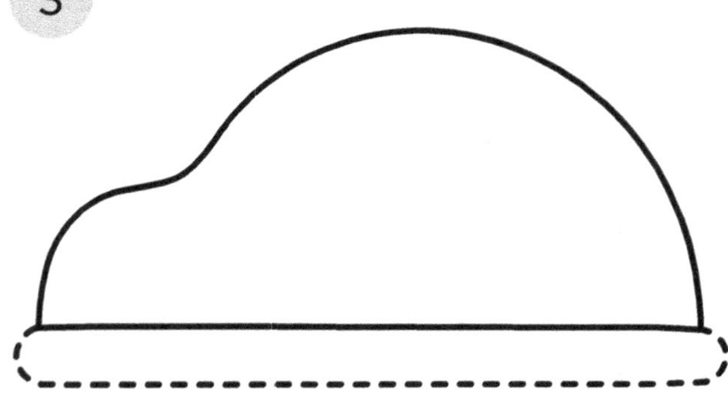

Draw a long rectangular tube

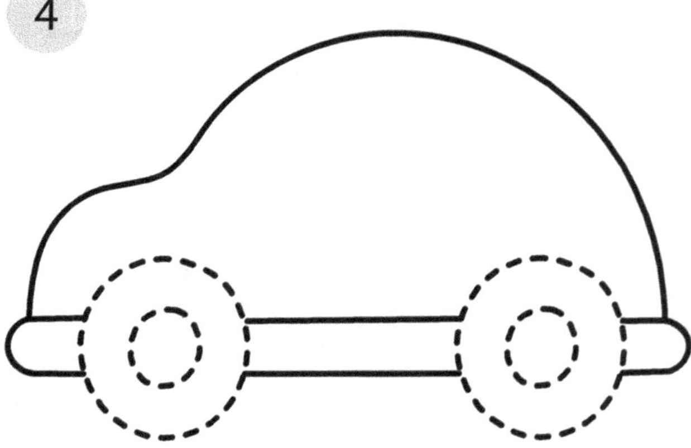

Now make two tires

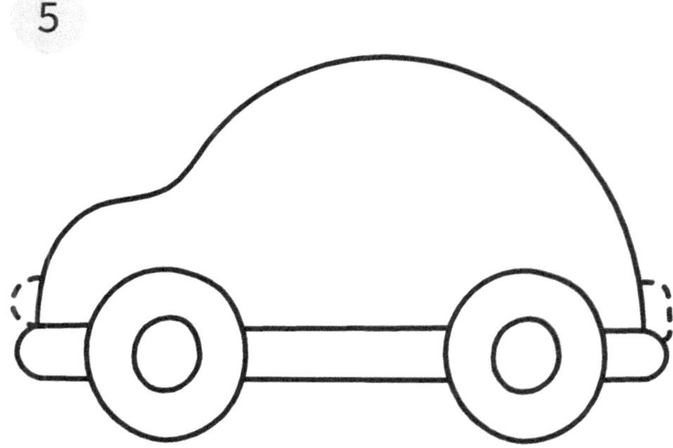

Draw the headlight and
tail light

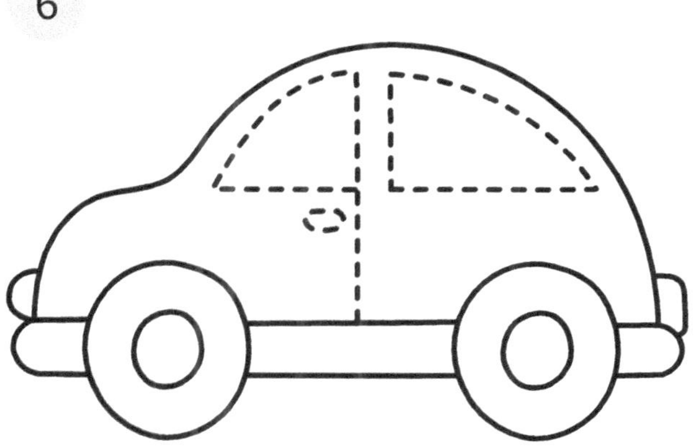

Make the windows
to complete your car!

MOTORCYCLE

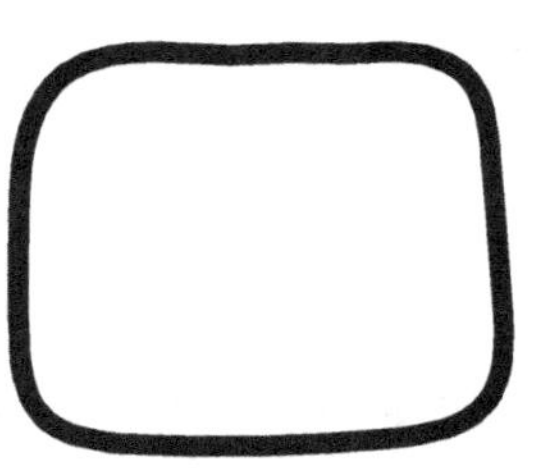

1 Draw a square
with round edges

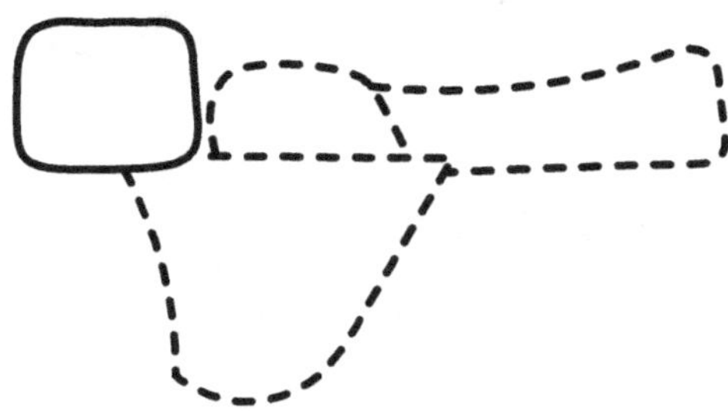

2 Draw a triangular
shape and the seat

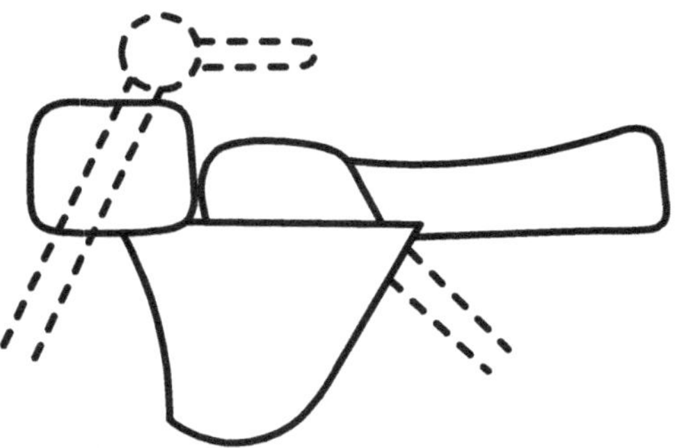

3 Draw the handle
and suspension

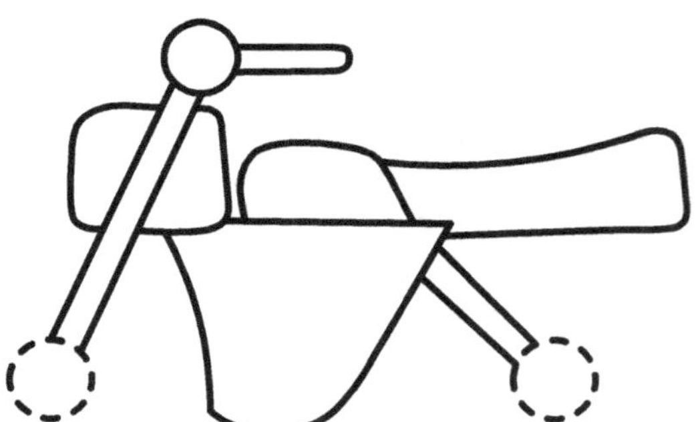

4 Draw two small circles

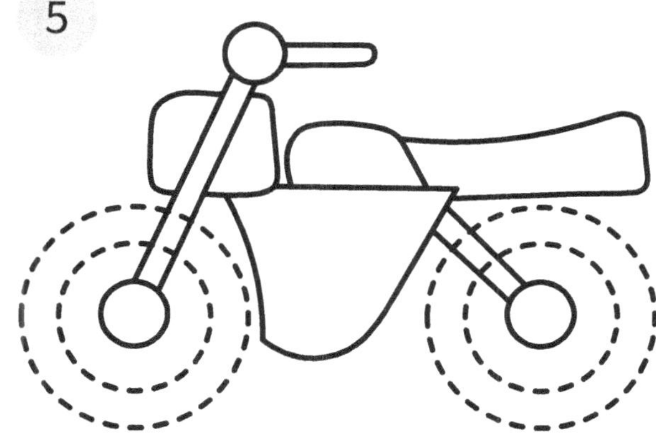

Draw two bigger concentric
circle for each wheel

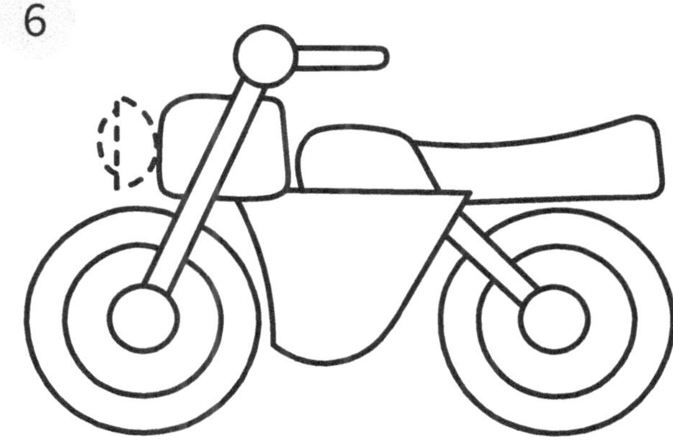

Draw the head light to
complete your motorcycle!

TRUCK

1 Start by drawing the driver's unit

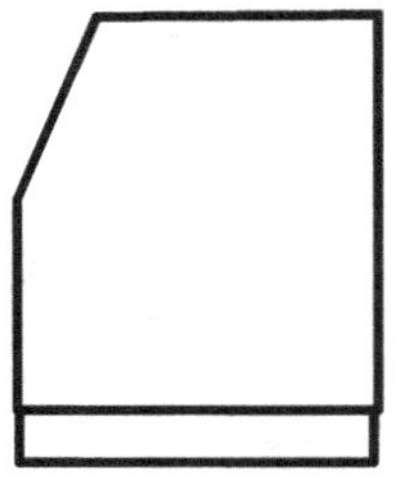

2 Draw a rectangular storage space

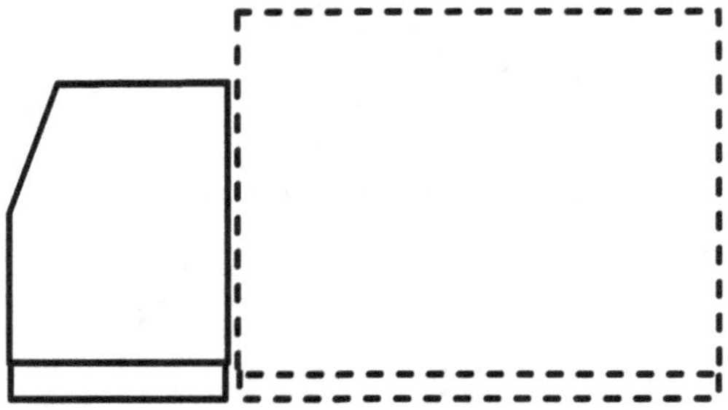

3 Draw two semi circles for the wheel sockets

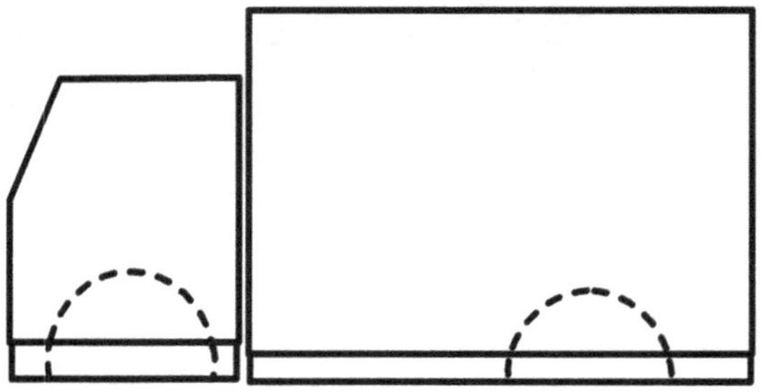

4 Draw two concentric circles for each wheel

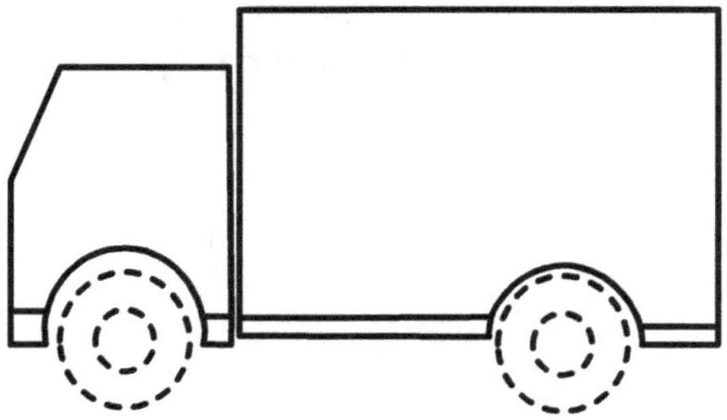

5 Draw the window and tail light to complete the truck!

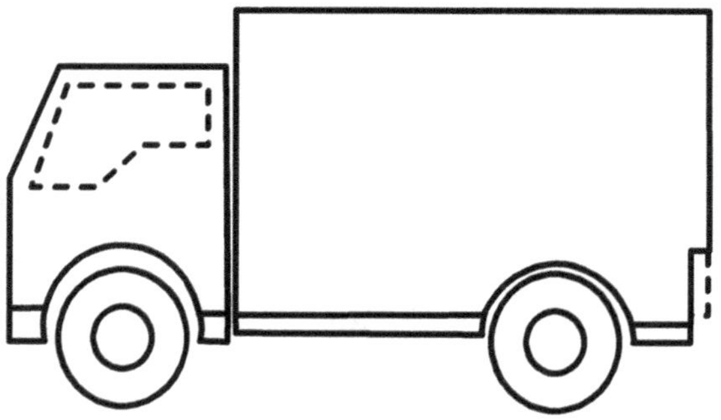

HELICOPTER

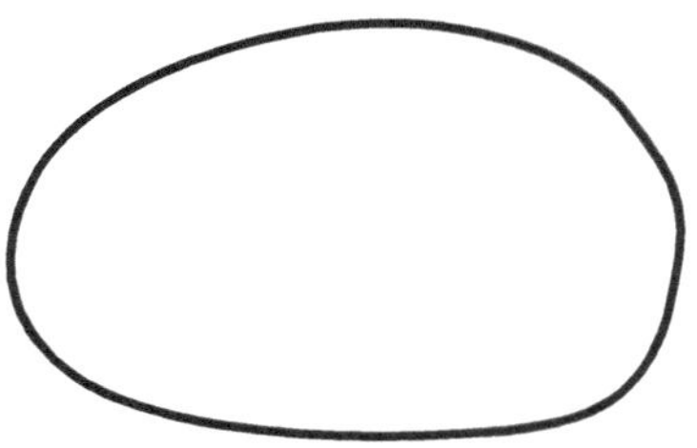

1

Draw an oval body

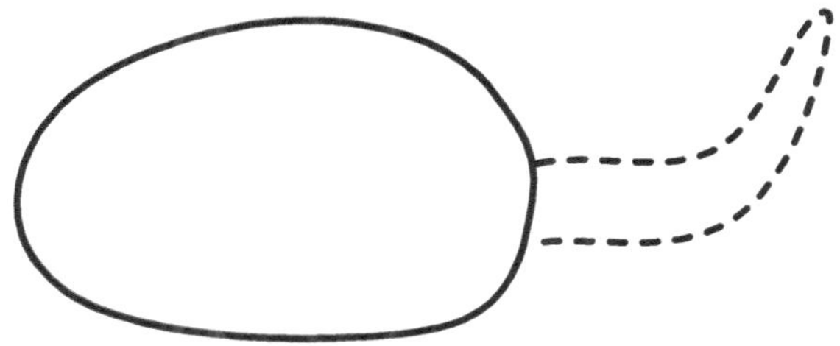

2

Make the tail
of the helicopter

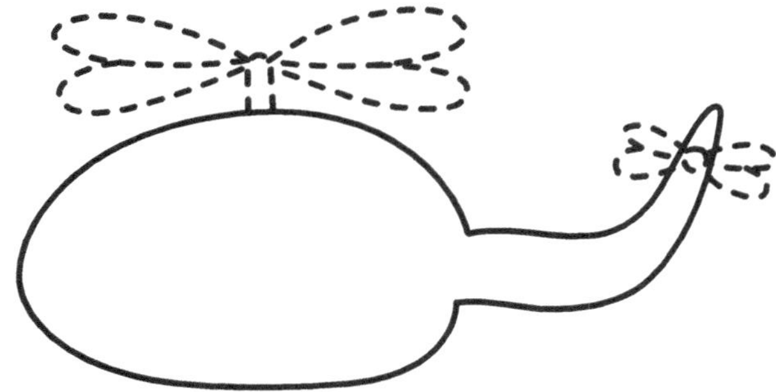

3

Draw the flying
blades of the helicopter

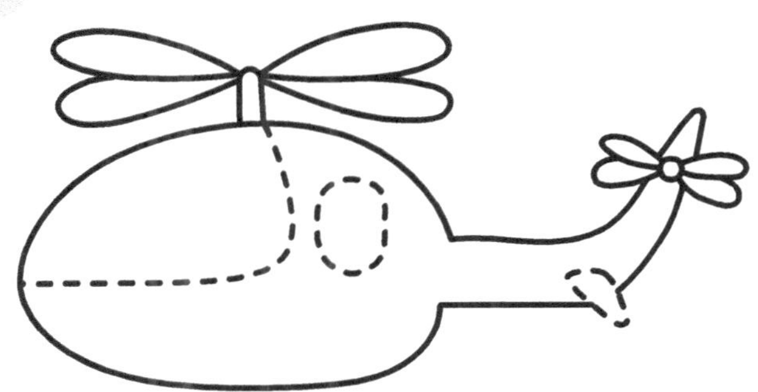

4

Add details to the helicopter

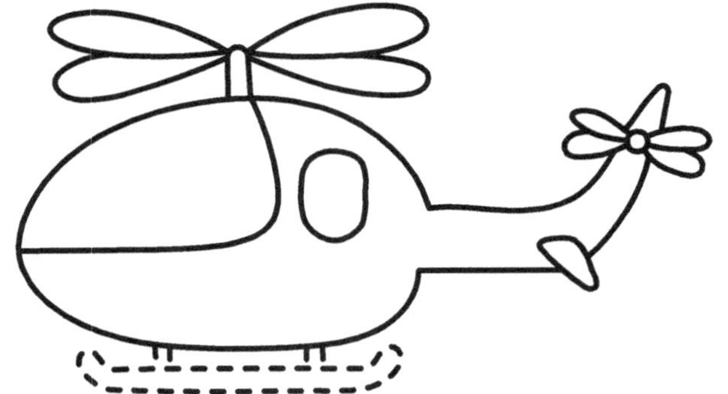

Make the landing skid

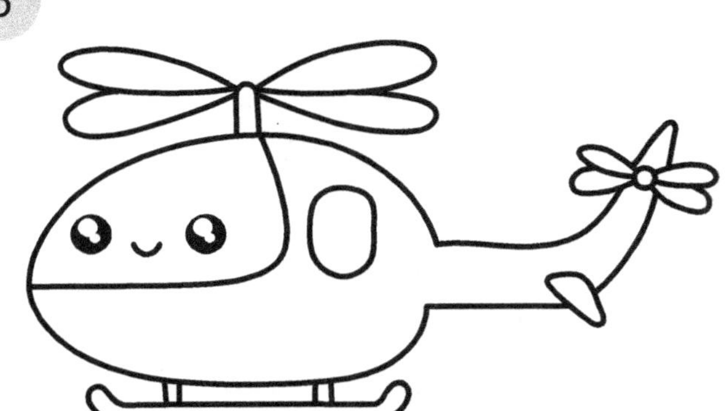

Draw the face to complete it!

AIRPLANE

1 Draw an oval body

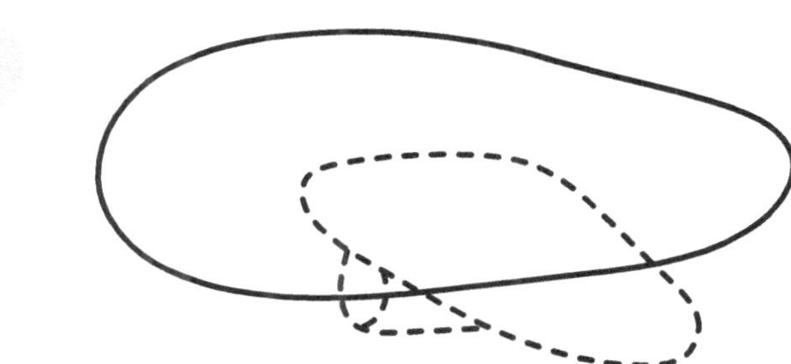

2 Draw the wing and the engine

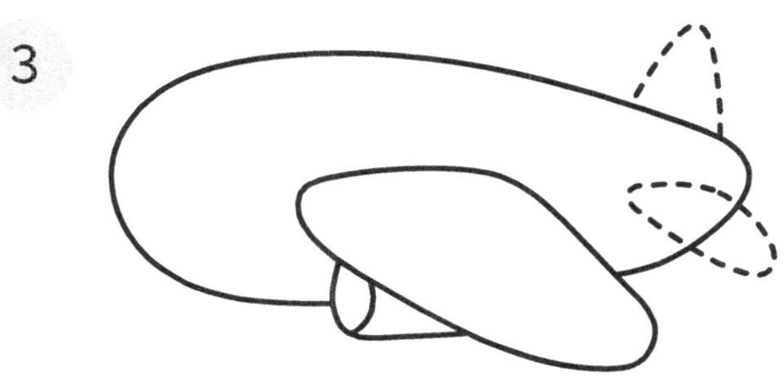

3 Make two tail wings

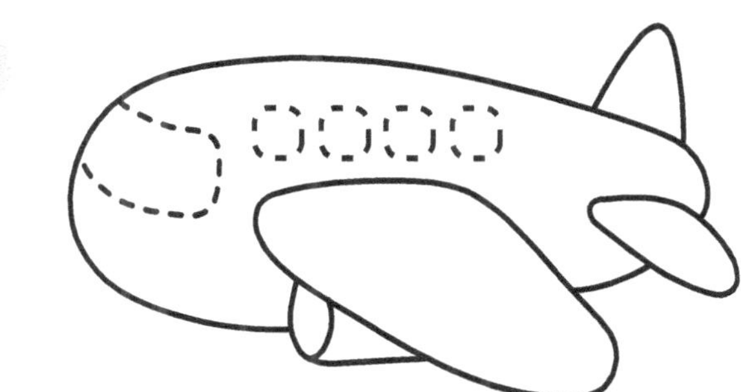

4 Make the windows and the windshield

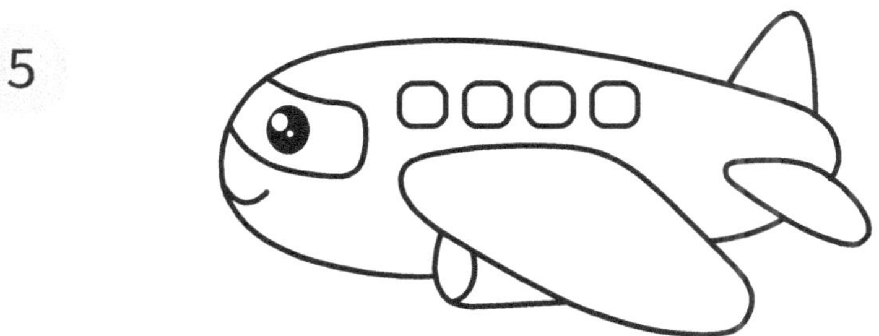

5 Draw the face to complete the airplane!

TRACTOR

1

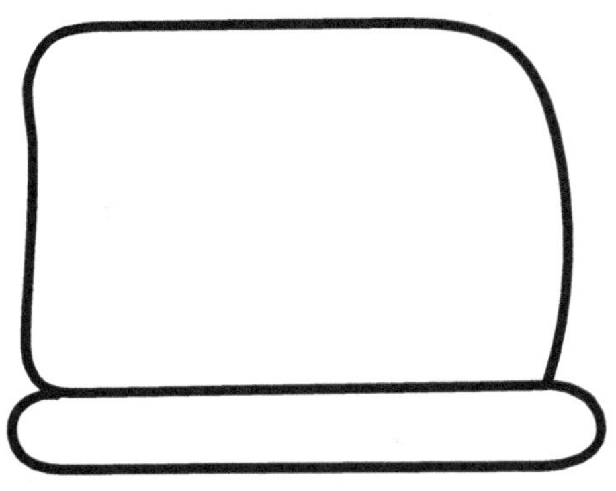

Start by drawing a
rectangle with curved edges

2

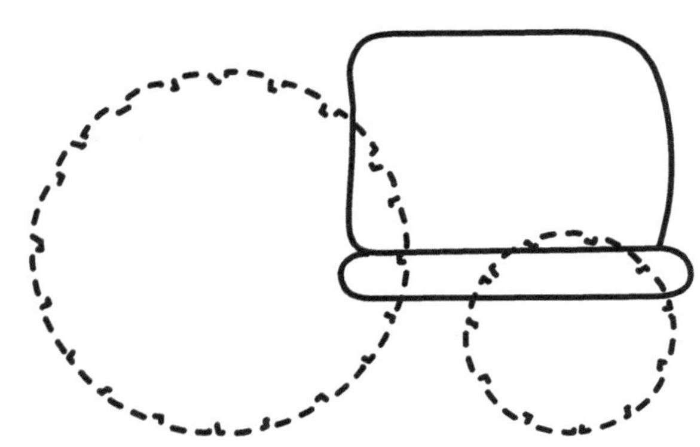

Draw two big tires

3

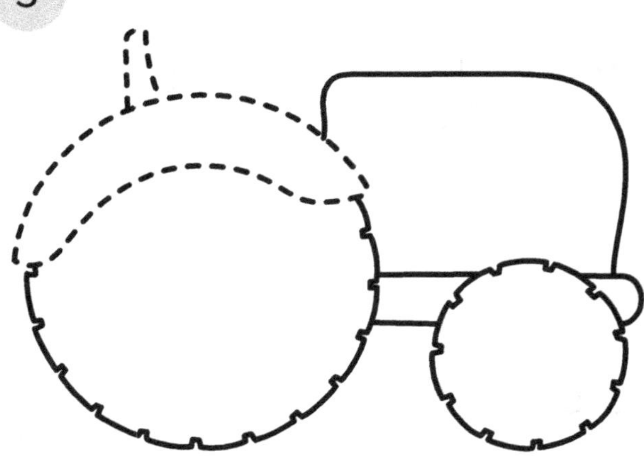

Draw the cover and the seat

4

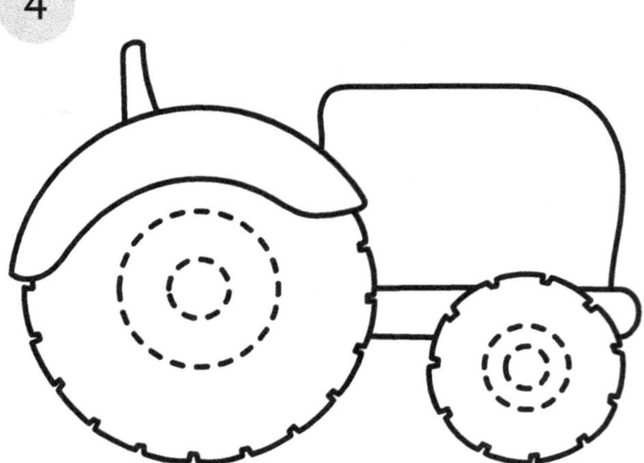

Make two more concentric
circles for each wheel

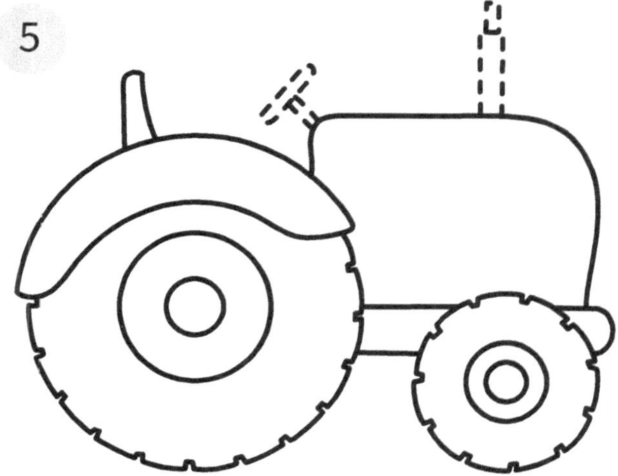

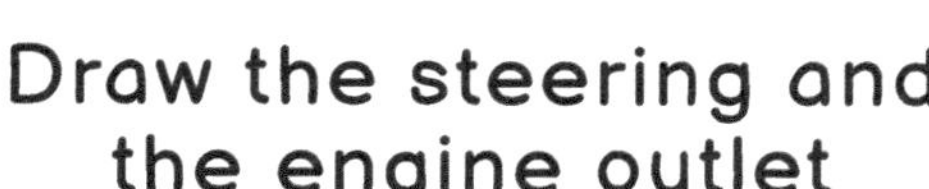

Draw the steering and
the engine outlet

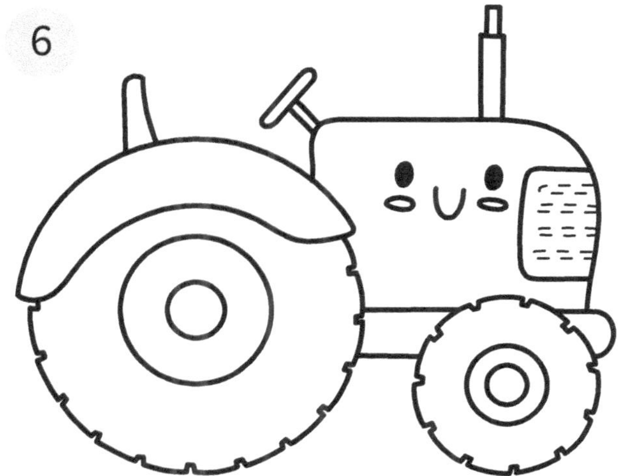

Make the face and
details to complete!

HOT AIR BALLOON

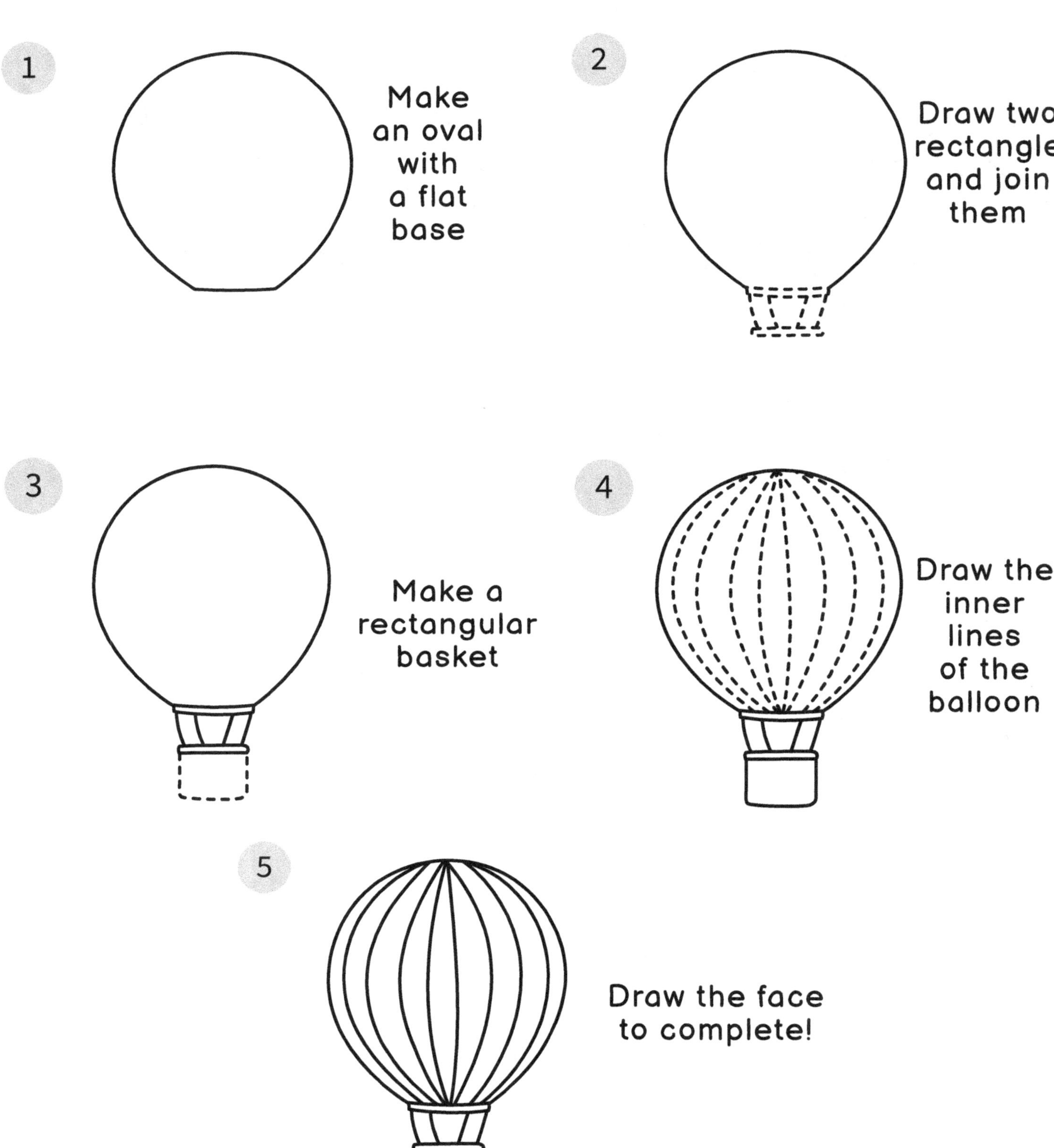

SPACESHIP

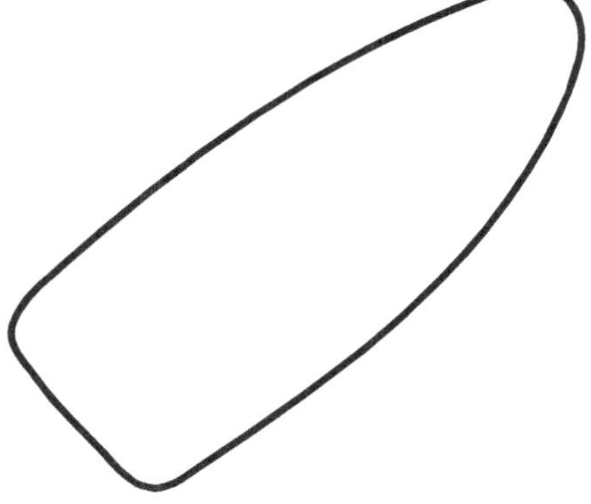

1

Start by drawing the body

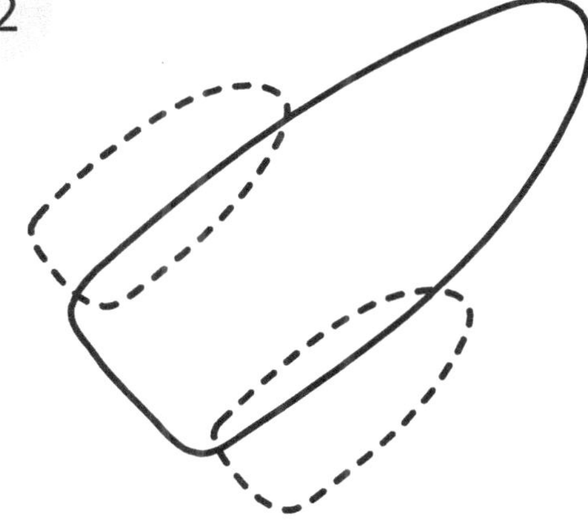

2

Draw two smaller ovals

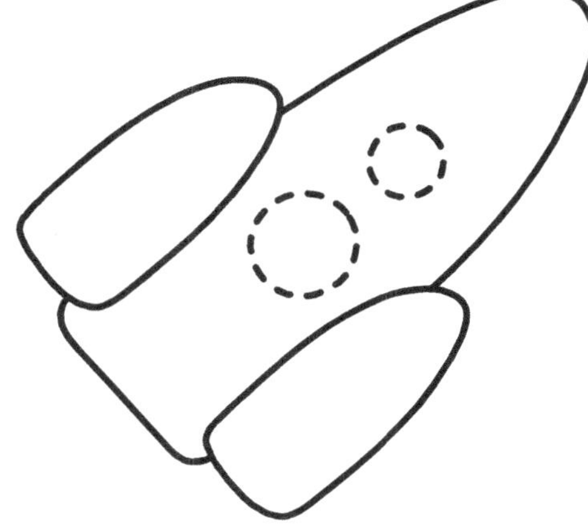

3

Draw two
circles for the windows

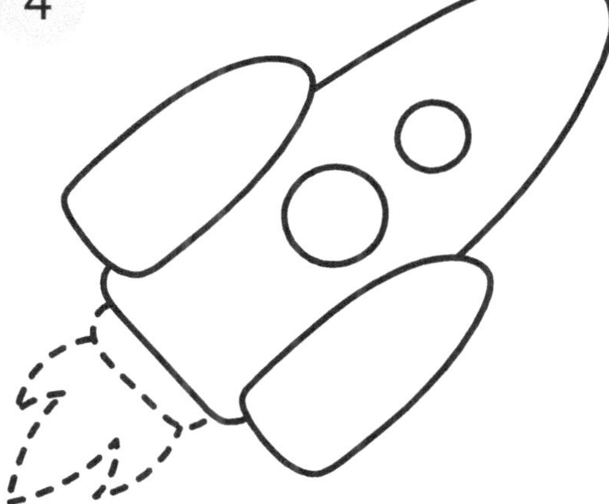

4

Draw the engine flame

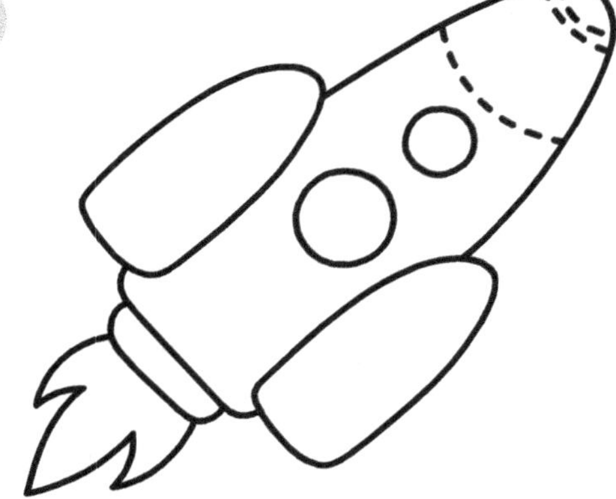

Draw the details

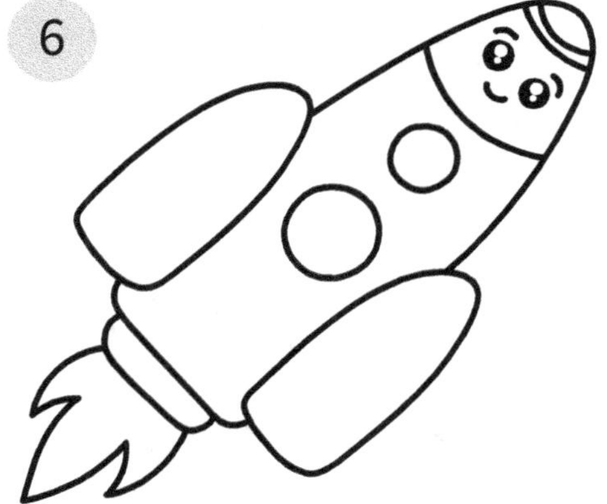

**Make a cute
face to complete!**

PLANET

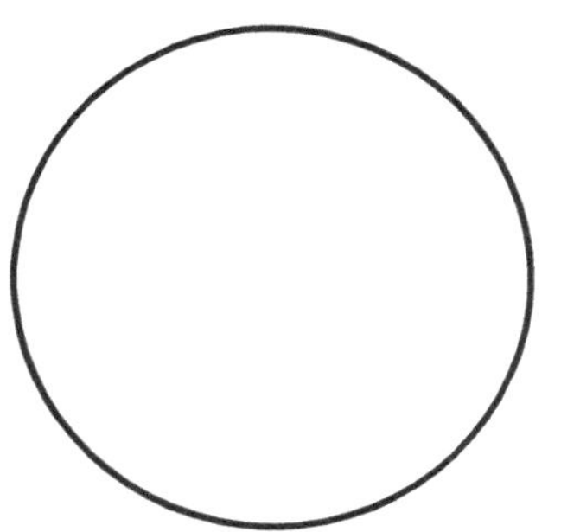

1

Draw a big circle

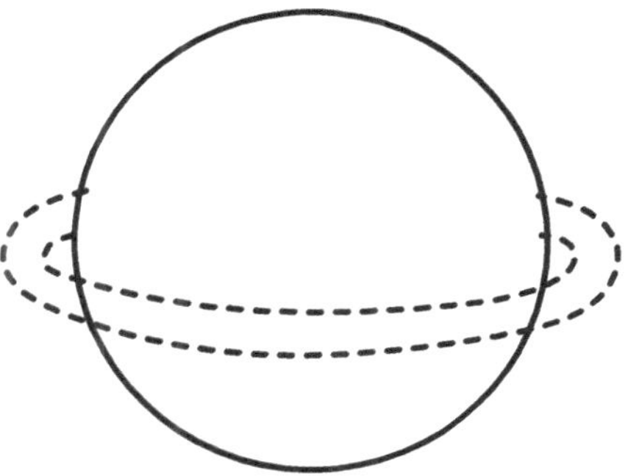

2

Draw a beautiful
ring around it

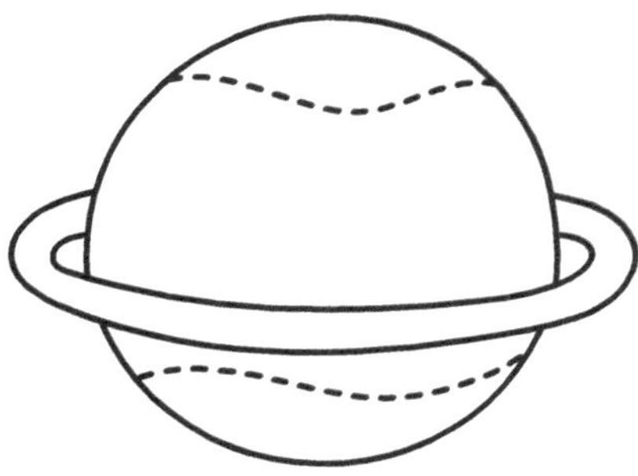

3

Make a pattern
on the planet

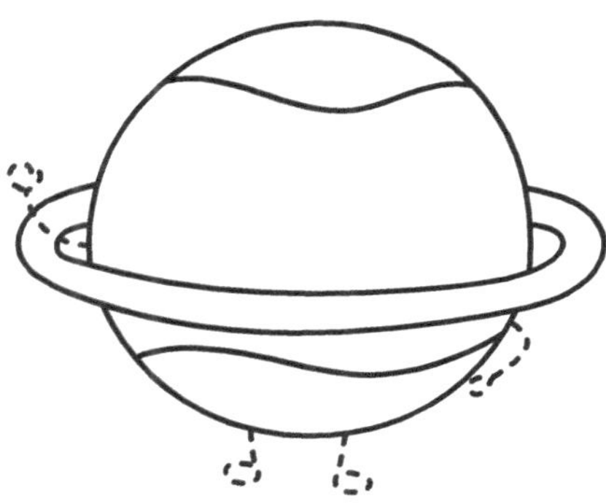

4

Draw cute arms and legs

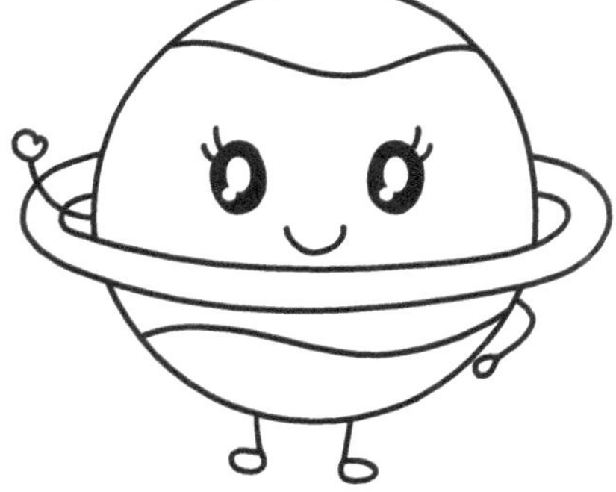

5

Draw an adorable
face to complete!

A Person

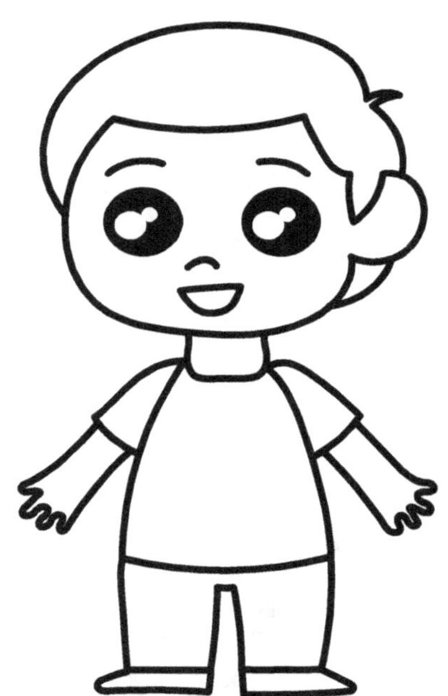

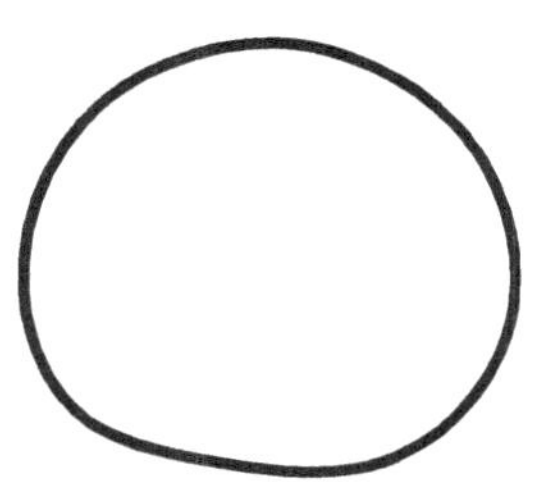

1

Draw a circular face

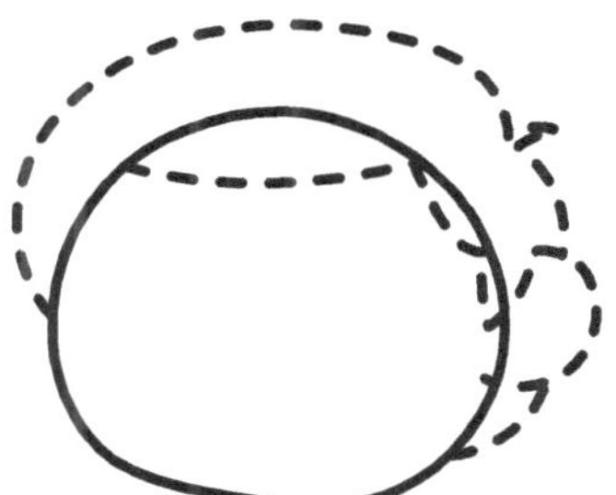

2

Draw the ear and hair

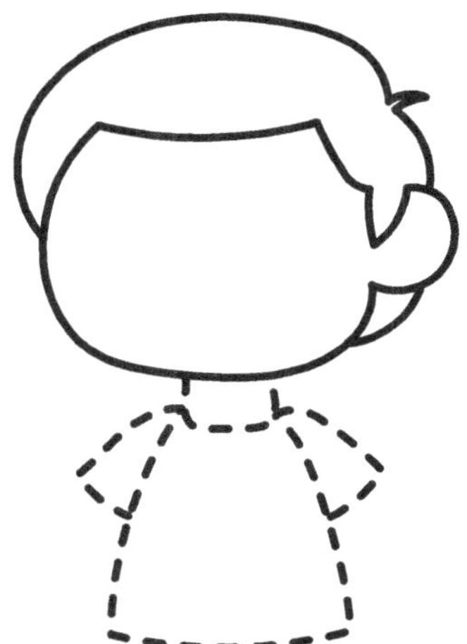

3

Make the neck
and the shirt

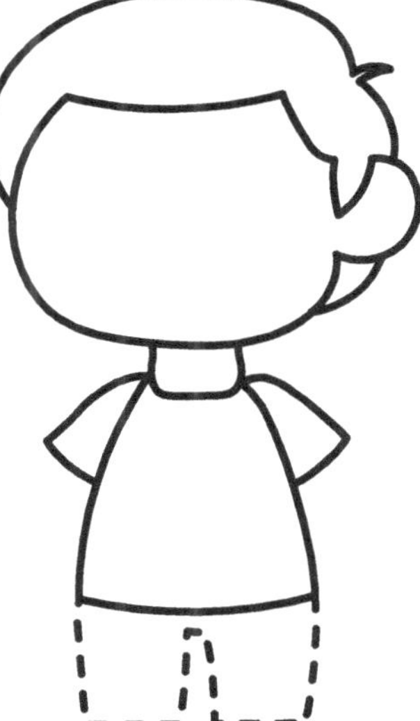

4

Draw two
rectangles for pants

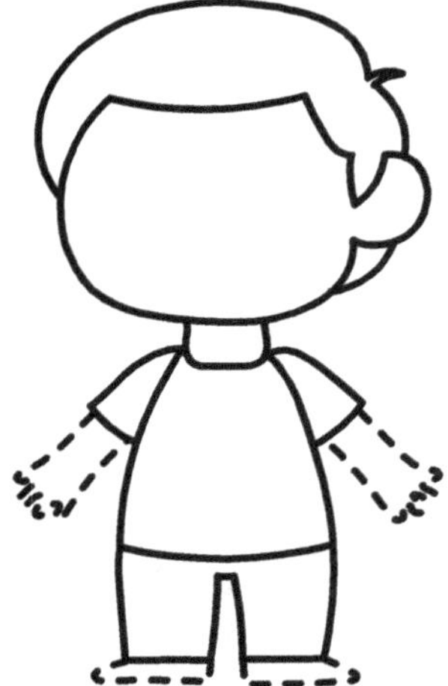

Draw the arms
and two shoes

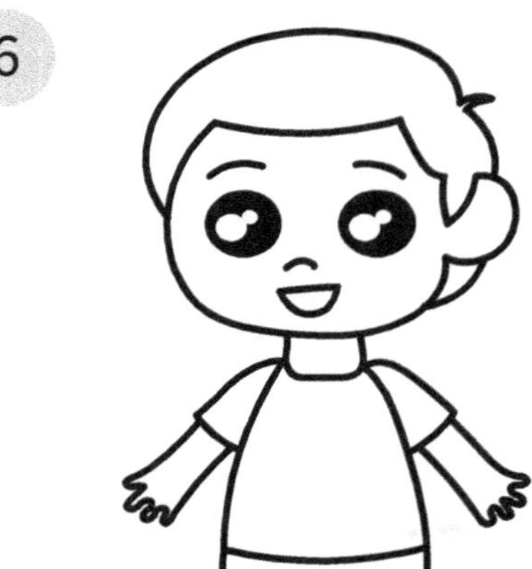

Make the face
to complete!

Thank you for getting our book!

If you find this drawing book fun and useful, we would be very grateful if you post a short review on Amazon! Your support does make a difference and we read every review personally.

If you would like to leave a review, just head on over to this book's Amazon page and click "Write a customer review".

Thank you for your support!